The 7th Floor
Ain't Too High for
Angels to Fly

The 7ᵗʰ Floor Ain't Too High for Angels to Fly

*A Collection of Stories
on Relationships
& Self-Understanding*

John M. Eades, Ph.D.

Health Communications, Inc.
Deerfield Beach, Florida

Library of Congress Cataloging-in-Publication Data

Eades, John M.
    The 7th floor ain't too high for angels to fly : a collection of
stories on relationships & self-understanding / John M. Eades.
        p. cm.
    ISBN 1-55874-356-1
    1. Self-help techniques. 2. Conduct of life. 3. Interpersonal
conflict. 4. Self-management (Psychology) I. Title.
    BF632.E19 1995
    158—dc20   95-24012
                                                        CIP

©1995 John M. Eades
ISBN 1-55874-356-1

Publisher: Health Communications, Inc.
                3201 S.W. 15th Street
                Deerfield Beach, Florida 33442-8190

Cover design by Andrea Perrine-Brower

Contents

Acknowledgments

I don't know if a chronological indebtedness is appropriate but it sure seems simpler. With this in mind, I wish to thank my "older" sister, Dianne, who says I *should* thank her for "letting me live when I was a boy." The smoke of sibling rivalry has long blown away and there isn't anything to compare with the love of a "big sister."

I am grateful for my wife, Karen, who has always believed in me. She has stood beside me, stood behind me, stood in front of me and even stood over me, but for some reason has never stood apart from me.

To Dana and Ginger, my daughters, I appreciate you two angels straining your wings to lift me to a higher plane, and you did.

I am sweetly indebted to all those people who inspired me by their faith and life experiences which they shared, especially Julie K.

To all the "paper trail" people, bless you. Wonderful David Colmans, who got the manuscript to Igor Cassini, a true Renaissance Man with great compassion and kindness, who took it to New York and agent Frank Weimann, who sent it to Peter Vegso, the publisher. Thank you all.

To my editor, Christine Belleris, you have been the flashlight at my feet guiding me through this process. I'm truly indebted.

To Sylvia Viator, my valued secretary, thank you for all your kindness and extra hours. Your assistance made the difference.

Oh yeah, thanks Mom for giving me life and love.

Introduction

If I were a pompous Ph.D., I might have written a book telling you what life is all about and how to fix yours in the event it is broken. Then I suppose I would have been presumptuous as well as pompous.

The truth is that I am educated well beyond my intelligence. In the jargon of the day I guess you might call me an overachiever. Of course, you might call anyone who does anything above grazing and sleeping the same thing. You see, what I really wanted to be was successful so I could feel good about myself. That might even be the case with you. Unfortunately, or fortunately, in the race for fame and fortune it seems, especially since I passed my fiftieth birthday, that I simply ran out of wind. Not only that, I was startled to find I had been running on the wrong track. So, metaphorically speaking, I have untied my tennis shoes and am sitting in the grass massaging my aching feet and silently cursing whoever it was that organized this stupid race in the first place. You see, one of the few smart things I have done in my life is realize there is no finish line to this race except death itself.

So, what am I telling you? I'm not presumptuous enough to tell you to stop striving for this imaginary finish line. I guess I'm just asking you to join me for a few hours of rest and reading, sitting here in the grass with your shoes off. You don't have to worry if your feet stink, everyone's feet stink, so it's okay.

If I could read these stories to you out loud, I would. They are stories written to be read that way. You might do that and be amazed to find you will know exactly where to put the emphasis as you read. Why is this?

I believe it's because I have written these stories from my soul to your soul. We all are more alike than different, especially in the sacred recesses of our souls. If you have struggled with life, if you are sensitive to your soul's longings, if you have that nagging feeling that something is missing in your life, if you're tired of striving and never arriving, then maybe, just maybe, these stories will touch you gently like an old friend.

As you read, I hope you will be enchanted, enlightened and encouraged. You see, through much trial and many errors, I realized it was time to slow down and catch up with my soul before I ran out of time. Aren't your feet tired?

A Charmed Life

Live each day as though it is
your last one—and
someday you will be right.

Unknown

Frank Thomas had always lived a charmed life. "Everything always turns up roses," he would smile and say when his predicaments would invariably dissolve into one lucky break or opportunity after another. Frank Thomas was indeed a charmed man; at least he was until that rainy day he sat across the desk from his doctor.

Frank's doctor shuffled through the stack of lab reports then looked directly at him. "Frank, your reports are bad. I'm going to be straight with you. You have an inoperable cancer with an outside chance to live six months." The doctor's eyes fixed briefly on the water beading on the window, then he closed the file as he looked back at Frank and said, "I'm sorry, there's nothing else we can do."

Frank exhaled and nodded his head in acknowledgment. A sardonic smile of resignation crossed his face as though he had become another victim of life's ongoing practical joke. Seconds longer than a lifetime passed before Frank stood to go. He shook the doctor's hand and vaguely understood why the Greeks killed the messenger who brought bad news.

The drive home was mostly a blur. He felt numb. A strange nostalgia would nibble briefly at his numbness, but for the most part he was insulated from the reality of his surroundings. He was in a stupor; he drove in a daze of instinct and habit until the car made its way into his driveway.

Weeks passed before Frank told his wife, Ellen. He had grown children, but he decided he would tell them later.

Slowly the emotional numbness began to lift like fog under a hot sun. Frank began to see things more clearly. Two nights after he had told Ellen the news, they were sitting at the cluttered kitchen table after dinner. Clean dishes had ceased to be one of Ellen's priorities.

Frank pushed his chair back from the table as he said, "I've made a decision, Ellen. We are going to spend whatever time is left together!" She leaned forward and touched his hand. "Whatever you want, Frank," she replied. "We'll do whatever you want. What do you want to do?"

"I want to sell the house, quit my job, and spend whatever time is left traveling the country with you. Don't you think it's about time we get to know each other again?" Frank asked with a faint, boyish smile.

Ellen's eyes said yes as Frank continued. "You know baby, I think I want to live before I die. I mean really live!" He jabbed his finger hard on the table for emphasis and then went on. "It seems we have just been existing for so long now. We haven't been living, just marking time like prisoners in the same cell. We've got to rediscover each other. Let's be better than Lewis and Clark. Let's discover new territory and each other at the same time. What do you say?"

For a long time Ellen didn't answer. She stared at Frank as though she were seeing him for the first time. "We've wasted too much precious time in the past, Frank, and there is no use in wasting any more. Time is too short. Let's do it!"

Some luck must have remained. The house sold in two weeks, the garage sale brought more ready cash, and they closed their savings accounts. The children thought their parents were going nuts. Frank and Ellen thought that at times, too. The departure day came. They waved good-bye to the house as they pulled out of the driveway to embark on their journey. Frank felt an eerie kind of peace and relief. It was indeed time to live.

The weeks and months flew by as they lived each day to its fullest. Sunsets and sunrises were too special for words. Frank and Ellen began to rediscover each other and felt the enthusiasm and exuberance of young lovers. They did it all: walked barefoot in the grass, tasted rain-drops on their tongues, smelled the sweet scents of mother earth, marvelled at God's creatures. They laughed as they threw their watches from Stone Mountain in Georgia. From now on, time was to be kept by their hearts and nature. Even traffic jams afforded them time to talk to each other as patience and tolerance grew, and what used to be important faded into insignificance. Often they wondered aloud why they had not lived life to its fullest before. Frank said it was ironic that getting the message about death had also brought the message about living life to the hilt.

Four months passed before they went back to tell their children the news about Frank's impending death. The children were sad, as expected, but all in all it was a meaningful final meeting. Everyone seemed tired, espe-cially the children, as some of them had driven so far from out of state to be there. Yet, they seemed to understand.

The next day Frank and Ellen were on the road again. Frank had ended his goodbyes to the children with, "Ellen won't be back until I'm dead." He felt at peace with the situation; emotionally and spiritually he was calm.

Two years have passed now. Two glorious life-filled years. Frank continues to believe that he is healing due to his healthier lifestyle. Ellen says it's the power of love.

The doctor had tried to telephone Frank many times,

but the phone number had long been "no longer in service." All the doctor's letters had been returned stamped "no forwarding address, return to sender."

If Frank ever had opened the doctor's letter, he would have thought he was in a scene from an old Frank Capra movie. It turns out the lab reports were in error. They weren't Frank Thomas' at all. They were Thomas Frank's, a gentle old man who is now dead.

If Frank Thomas had stayed at his old address, his friends certainly would be saying today that he was a man who always had lived a charmed life. He never got the news of the medical mistake. Come to think of it, Frank Thomas *is* a man living a truly charmed life.

Gone to See Nora

The most I ever did
for you was to outlive you.
But that was much.

Edna St. Vincent Millay

A gaunt man with long gray hair sat on a park bench feeding squirrels. He looked as though he should have been eating the popcorn himself from the way his much too large overcoat and shirt hung like Spanish moss from his fragile frame. He smiled a proud father's smile at the squirrels gathered at his feet for their daily feeding. He was as much a part of the park as the old metal water fountain with the sticking pedal, and his words trickled down gently to his frisky friends.

"Tomorrow is the day," he said as he reached into the wrinkled brown paper sack for more popcorn. "Tomorrow my kids are going to pick me up in their new car to take me to Serenity Forest where they'll deposit me like they do money in a bank account."

The squirrels rose to their hind feet, anticipating the fluffy kernels in his hand. "Ah, my friends, you want to know what Serenity Forest is? Well, it's a retirement home, although it sure isn't my home. My home is over there." He nodded his head in the direction of the small white house that was on the border of the park. "They figure I'm too old to live by myself, and they're afraid I might hurt myself. They don't want me to live with them because I might hurt them by hindering their social climbing."

He tossed the popcorn with his words. "I'm not sure where they're climbing, but I reckon I'd be slowing them down. They aren't old enough to realize nothing is up there, and they aren't wise enough to come back down." The squirrels held the popcorn between their front feet, munching and staring attentively at him. He gave a wistful chuckle as he said, "Sometimes I'm sure you understand me a lot better than my children do."

The old man whistled a tune that lived long before transistors and stared down at his empty hands. They were as wrinkled and worn as the old paper sack containing the popcorn. Now he seemed to speak more to himself than to the squirrels.

"These hands held three children and a wife for many years. These hands were dipped in dreams until they were soaked with love and hope for the future. They used to hug Nora so tight she'd laugh and say she'd never get my fingerprints off her heart." He questioned the sky, "God, Nora, why did you have to die and leave me with such lonely hands?"

Finally, he glanced back down at his hands. "These hands were once strong and smooth and sent the children soaring up into the air on Saturday afternoons, and caught them as they screamed their special squeals of fear and fun on the way down. They pushed swings high enough to kiss God, and held the children up to that old water fountain right over there." He nodded toward the fountain as though the squirrels really could understand him.

"These hands built doll houses and dog houses so my daughter and two sons could learn to care for others. I wish I could have bottled all the love that flowed from them to the baby dolls and puppies. I'd just turn it up and pour it all over me right now. That's what I'd do all right."

His hands massaged each other as though he could push the arthritis out of his fingers to ease the stiffness and soreness.

He turned the sack of popcorn upside down and shook it empty for the squirrels. He stood to leave, but the squirrels made no effort to move. They knew he wouldn't step on them or hurt them. He had fed them every day now for almost ten years.

That night he climbed into the bed he had shared with Nora for over 40 years. He had sprayed the back of his hand with the Avon perfume she always wore. He smelled and smiled and listened as though any moment Nora would come through the house and appear in the doorway to the bedroom.

He looked again at his hands. The hands that hours ago held popcorn now were holding a glass of water and a mound of pills.

The morning brought the sun, the squirrels and the old man's sons. Young hands clutched the note written by old hands. It read, "Gone to see Nora."

A gaunt woman with long gray hair sat on the park bench feeding the squirrels. She looked like she should have been eating the popcorn herself . . .

You Can't Fly with Only One Wing

People who suffer from
"I" trouble have a
difficult time seeing what
really matters.

Unknown

Me-ism is alive and sick. "Look out for number one." "It's a dog-eat-dog world (by the way, humans are the only mammals who abuse their young)." "Every man for himself." "Do unto others before they do it to you." "Do your own thing." "Follow the new Golden Rule, which really means those who have the gold make the rules." The many cliches of Me-ism.

Business is brisk at sporting events for those giant styrofoam hands with the "number one" finger pointing at the sky. Maybe the "I"s have it or, more accurately, have us.

Goethe wrote the masterful dramatic poem, *Faust.* Faust, perhaps the original yuppie, was a man who sold his soul to the devil in exchange for just one moment on earth so fulfilling that he would finally say, "Let this moment linger, it is so good."

The devil gives Faust everything he desires, but Faust is a selfish man, and difficult to satisfy. He has wealth, women, power and status, but he still feels empty. Only near the end of his life, when Faust is helping to build dikes for poor farmers, does he for the first time say, "Let this moment linger, it is so good." Faust finally finds himself by losing himself in concern for the welfare of others.

Carl Jung, the brilliant psychiatrist and contemporary of Freud, said in his book, *Modern Man in Search of a Soul,* "About a third of my cases are suffering from no clinically definable neurosis, but from the senselessness and emptiness of their lives."

Appearance seems so important these days. Narcissus, the Greek myth tells us, fell in love with his own reflection in the water, but never loved anyone else. Our cultural myths promoted by Madison Avenue hucksters tell us it's what's on the outside that counts. They have sold us a cup with a hole in it, and enough is never enough to fill it up. Yet, we have learned to define ourselves by those things outside ourselves.

Our myths are CDs, careers, condos, cars, college degrees, checking accounts, cosmetic surgery and cellular phones. Do these outside things really tell us who we are? Do they really make us happy? Maybe the sweet smell of success is simply the early odor of the soul rotting. Why are we surprised when "success" kisses us back with dry lips?

It seems we are supposed to use things and love people instead of the other way around. The beast in Madame de Villeneure's *Beauty and the Beast* remarks, "There is many a monster with the form of a man. It is the better of the two to have the heart of a man and form of a monster." Isn't it what's on the inside that counts?

There is a terrific story about a man who dies and wakes up in Hell. Satan takes him into a room where he smells a wonderful stew being cooked. In the middle of the room, he sees a giant cooking kettle with people seated all around it.

The man hears their moaning and sees their horribly gaunt bodies, bones protruding like the starving Jews in the German prison camps. They are moaning from hunger, and tears drip down their bony cheeks.

The new arrival notices they all have long ladle-like spoons dipped into the stew. The ladles are tied to their hands, and though they can dip the stew they cannot eat because the ladles are too long to get the food into their mouths.

"Please," said the man, "show me what I missed. Show me Heaven."

"What's a few moments out of eternity," said Satan as he took the man over to Heaven.

The man was amazed and confused. It was the same scene he had seen in Hell except these people were happy, healthy and laughing. "I don't understand," he said. "It's the same thing. People with long ladle-like spoons tied to their hands sitting around a kettle of stew. What's the difference? Why is this Heaven?"

Satan didn't answer and began to lead him from the room. As they neared the door, the man looked over his shoulder just in time to see the answer—they were feeding each other!

Perhaps John Donne, the poet, was right when he said that no man is an island, and we need not ask for whom the bell tolls, it tolls for us. We really *are* all a part of the whole and *do* need each other. Maybe to find meaning we must just lose the "me."

Jesus, in his divine wisdom, narrowed it down to two great commandments. One was to love God with all our being, and the other was to love our neighbors as ourselves.

Our task is to help, not hurt. To lift up, not to put down. As Luciano De Croscengo says, "We are each of us angels with only one wing. And we can only fly embracing each other."

It's Christmas Day for Those Who Believe in Santa

First there is a time when we believe everything without reasons, then for a little while we believe with discrimination, then we believe nothing whatever, and then we believe everything again—and moreover, give reasons why we believe everything.

Christopher Lichtenberg

t was a strange sight. The long line inched its way through the gigantic department store as people waited to see Santa Claus. It wouldn't have been such an unusual sight except for one small thing—all the people standing in the line were adults. Funny how if you look closely at adult faces at Christmas time, you still can see the little boys and girls hidden behind the wrinkles and crowsfeet and the other facial burdens that come as the price of being big and supposedly responsible. It seems pressure just isn't the best playmate to have.

So they stood. Their eyes had lost that cloudy look caused by life's storms and they shined brightly with optimism and hope. That's the way it was this particular night. Grown men and women lined up, waiting for their turn to sit on Santa's lap. It was more than just a strange sight, it turned out to be a *mighty* strange night or at least that's what Uncle Bill said. Uncle Bill was there, and he never lied.

He said it seemed as if he'd been standing in line for hours, but he didn't care because his legs weren't getting tired. Finally, he was first in line. He waited patiently at the foot of the escalator that went up to the next floor where Santa was.

"What kind of questions will he ask?" Uncle Bill inquired of Pete, one of Santa's main helpers, who was posted at the foot of the escalator and seemed to be in charge of crowd control and giving the okay to step on the moving stairs.

"Oh, nothing big," came Pete's cheery reply. "Probably

something simple like, 'Have you been a good man this year?'"

"That's a pretty childish question," Uncle Bill replied. "Don't you think he'll ask something more complicated than that?"

"Nope," Pete grinned. "He likes to ask simple questions. Sometimes he'll ask if you've been kind to the homeless, or petted a stray dog, or given food to a hungry person, or dropped a dollar in a beggar's cup. Let me see," Pete thought as he scratched his head. "I remember last year one of his favorite questions was whether you had given someone clothes to keep them warm."

"I do that every year." Uncle Bill brightly answered. "Why, last year I gave several of my old suits to the Salvation Army."

A frown grew across Pete's forehead. "I don't think he means that kind of giving. I believe he wants to know if you've directly given someone something to wear. You know, like meeting someone who is cold and giving them something to wear right then. That kind of thing."

"Oh," Uncle Bill replied. "I see what you mean." He felt a little embarrassed and looked down at his feet.

"Now, now," Pete chimed up, "don't fret so much, no one's perfect."

Uncle Bill looked back up at Pete. "Where's the down escalator? I haven't seen anybody come back down once they've seen Santa, and a lot of people have gone up there." He pointed toward the top of the escalator.

Pete smiled and whispered as if telling a secret, "It's on the other side."

Uncle Bill thought for a moment and then asked Pete, "Isn't it unusual that you're open this late on Christmas Eve?"

"Nope," Pete answered with a laugh. "We're open every day of the year."

"Even on Christmas Day?" Bill asked with wide eyes that made him look every bit of seven years old rather than 57.

"Especially on Christmas Day," Pete said with a sincere smile. "That's his favorite day of the year," he said as he tossed a knowing look toward the top of the escalator.

"Why is it taking so long?" Uncle Bill asked, glancing nervously at his watch. "It's after midnight: it's already Christmas Day, and here I am standing in line to see Santa. I think I'd better be going home. My family will be waiting."

"Don't worry, Bill," Pete said, "they know you're here. In fact, the man upstairs knows you're here." Pete looked up toward the top of the escalator again. "He's been waiting to see you. Besides, it's just about time for your ride up to see him. You do believe in him, don't you?"

"Of course I do," Uncle Bill said, as he looked behind him at the line with no end. "How many people does he see?" Uncle Bill asked as he continued to stare at the river of people behind him.

"Oh, he sees everybody," Pete chuckled, "but now it's your turn." He gently took Uncle Bill's hand and led him on to the escalator.

Uncle Bill said it was the greatest thing that ever happened to him. It was the happiest night of his life, but he always seemed the happiest when he said he never did find the down escalator.

I awoke to the smell of hot coffee. The dream is always the same. It's almost like he was with me, and it seems the echo of his voice fades just as I open my eyes. Uncle Bill died on Christmas Day in 1963. He sure was a good man. He always said Christmas Day was for those who still believed in Santa Claus.

Aunt Gertrude's Letter

To err is human, to
forgive divine.

Alexander Pope

Mike's Aunt Gertrude stood on the front porch holding her paisley canvas bag in one hand and that navy blue metal carrying case in the other. The veins in her arms stood out in relief just like the mountain ranges on Billy Cobb's expensive globe of the world. Billy was Mike's best friend in grade school long before Mike discovered the word "best" wasn't necessary when describing a friend. Then there was Aunt Gertrude. She was Mike's next "best" friend, and her annual spring visit always prompted his sapling soul to bud with joy. This visit was special because this was the year it would all happen.

Mike always felt special because he was the one Aunt Gertrude always asked to carry her paisley bag into the house. However, she was very particular about that navy blue carrying case, and never allowed anyone to tote it but herself.

One year she had just arrived and was busy talking to Mike's mother on the front porch when Mike picked up the navy case. It seemed heavy; so heavy he couldn't believe she could lift it, much less carry it. When Aunt Gertrude saw him, she quickly took it from him and admonished him to never do that again. Mike didn't, but at least he now knew why the veins in her right arm were so big—what he didn't know was what that blue case contained.

Each year after Aunt Gertrude left, Mike would get together with his friend Billy and they would try to guess what she had in that blue case. They agreed it must be a mighty big secret, and their curiosity grew to be almost unbearable.

Often they spent hours talking about what they thought was in that well-guarded blue case. Billy said old maids like Aunt Gertrude were just naturally weird, and he bet the case contained the bones of all her dead cats. Mike said he thought the case probably was filled to the brim with souvenirs of all her travels. Whatever was in there, they had determined that this would be the year the mystery would be solved. Mike would be the spy. He'd look inside the blue case and report back to Billy.

Finally, the morning came when Mike's mother and Aunt Gertrude left to go shopping for the day. Mike went into the bedroom where Aunt Gertrude slept, and pulled the blue case out from underneath the bed. He thought his heart would burst from his chest when he flicked the metal catches and the case popped open. Mike couldn't believe his eyes. He rummaged through the contents, then closed the case and replaced it exactly where he had found it.

He ran to Billy's house with guilt chasing after him. Mike felt more like Judas than James Bond, but most of all he felt confused about the contents of the blue case.

Billy couldn't believe it when Mike caught his breath and began to tell him what he had found. Even when Mike repeated it again clearly it didn't make much sense. Mike told him he had found a pair of heavy metal leg braces, the kind children used to wear if they had polio. Mike said he also found a lot of heavy rocks wrapped in toilet paper and an envelope, which he was afraid to remove, taped to the inside of the case. Mike wished he had never opened the blue case, but he felt compelled to understand what it all meant.

With Billy tagging along for added courage, they went back to Mike's house. This time Mike removed the envelope from the case. They pulled the letter from the envelope as though it was a lost scroll. Their lives would never be the same since they now had the burden of carrying a secret.

The letter was written by Gertrude's mother, Mike's grandmother, who had died before Mike was born. All he knew about her was that his father said she was the most special mother in the world. The letter read:

> *Dear Gertrude,*
>
> *I love you so very much my darling daughter.*
>
> *I pray that you will stop punishing yourself. I also pray that your father will come to his senses. He was so foolish to tell you he would never speak to you again. He is such a stubborn man and his pride often seems more powerful than his love. Maybe it is. But he is wrong.*
>
> *Your son did not die from polio because he was born out of wedlock. You were a good mother and it was a bad virus that killed him. You must stop punishing yourself by carrying this burden every day.*
>
> *Gertrude, you know my favorite Bible verse is when Jesus says, "Let him who is without sin cast the first stone." I have no stones, just love for you.*
>
> *Please write soon. There is no need for penance. I long to see you. I miss you so much.*
>
> I love you,
Mom

Mike gently folded the letter and put it back in the envelope. Why the stones?

That was the day someone cut the screen door, broke into Mike's house, and stole Aunt Gertrude's blue metal case. It was also the day Mike cast the first stone—into the creek that ran behind the neighborhood.

Gentle into That Good Night

Forgiveness is the answer to the
child's dream of a miracle by
which what is broken is made
whole again, what is soiled is
again made clean.

Dag Hammarskjöld

It was late. It was a time when I was doing private practice counseling in the evening: that time before I discovered I was killing myself making a living; a time before I found out that psychotherapy was often a fancy word for honest, heart-to-heart talk.

He had come for counseling, and the darkness of the night followed the man and his mood into my office. His face was lined and his faded eyes sunk deep in dark circles; he had the look of a man who had survived a tragedy, but who wished he had died because the memories were more brutal than the tragic moment. Something had killed a part of him, and sardonic fate had left the other part alive to know it. The rains of reality had eroded the soil of his spirit. I knew this night I would journey with him through the barren wasteland of his mind where only thoughts with thorns could survive.

He told me what had brought him to see me. It took 30 minutes and forever. His daughter had committed suicide. I heard his words, lifeless, as though emotional euthanasia had already been performed. Now, we sat in silence as the clock ticked loudly.

He stared down at the floor as if the answer to his torment was buried somewhere deep in the intricate weave of the carpet. It appeared that even his body had surrendered to gravity as his shoulders sagged lower. Then it happened.

This weary Atlas, crushed by carrying the burden of his world, wept. The tears streamed down the crevices of his wrinkled face, overflowed, and ran through the parched gullies of his soul. The truth rushed after the tears. His 17-year-old daughter, carrying an envelope and fear, had come to see him one night last week and told him she was pregnant. He had wanted her to be perfect, not pregnant. In a rage, he tore up the envelope, threw the pieces in her face, and angry words followed. "You make me sick. You have disgraced this family. Get out of my sight; I can't stand to look at you. Pick up every piece of that paper and go to your room."

That night, alone in the silence of her dark bedroom and the loudness of her self-hate, a senseless decision was made. The scissors were sharp, her skin was soft, and her breath and blood left her and went "gentle into that good night." A fragile child, a blood sacrifice to her earthly god.

They found her the next morning. There next to the headboard, now her wooden tombstone, was a card she had bought the day before. The pieces had carefully been taped together. The card simply read, "Happy Father's Day."

We left together, two large silhouettes with two small spirits. We stood by our cars, awkward and aching. He said he would call and make another appointment, but we both knew we would not meet again. He said he was going to make an effort to call his minister, and we both knew he would. As we shook hands good night, I realized his handshake was stronger than before. His voice was steady when he told me his wife had been pregnant with his daughter when they had married. His mask had melted.

As he unlocked his car, he turned and said, "Doctor, right now I don't see any good that can come from this tragedy, but if you ever think it would help other parents to be gentle and loving with their children, feel free to tell them about me." Well, I've told you. I knew he wouldn't go "gentle into that good night."

The Night
the Statues Moved

There is a time for
departure even when there's
no certain place to go.

Tennessee Williams
Camino Real

The small, quaint southern town evoked pleasant memories of simpler times. There was a park that covered a whole city block right in the center of town. It was surrounded by a white courthouse, the post office, a grand historic home and a most impressive bank building. In front of the buildings were freshly painted cannons and statues of famous people. The statues were like giant chess pieces frozen in time in the eternal stalemate between the old and the new. The cannons suggested the old saying, "all's fair in love and war," as deeply carved lovers' initials could still be seen beneath the fresh paint.

The park was beautiful with thick green grass and trees older than resentments. There were park benches of wood and concrete, and cobblestone walkways that all led to the big wooden gazebo in the middle of the park. Beside the gazebo stood a wooden bandstand. The crisp air was a reminder that it was almost time for the annual Autumn dance, which took place here in the park. Soon people would be dancing beneath the wooden dome of the gazebo.

From a distance, the people dancing inside the gazebo would resemble a magical music box with moving figurines. At least that was the way it always looked to Evoli Jones, who had always stood across the street whenever the Autumn dance was taking place. He loved the big globe lights in the park that cast their romantic rays down upon the crowd.

Last year, like every year, Evoli had watched the dance from the post office steps. The post office was his favorite building and he went there every day to see if there was any mail from his parents. The postmistress would pretend to search through her stacks of mail, then shake her head and tell him "maybe tomorrow." He was not discouraged, but the postmistress was because she knew the truth just like Evoli's grandma knew the truth—his parents were never going to write. He lived with his grandma because his parents had abandoned him when he was four years old and had left it up to her to raise him.

Fifteen years had passed since then, but Evoli wasn't too good at understanding time. In fact, there were a lot of things he couldn't understand. Evoli was retarded.

His face was as dark as the night sky with eyes as bright as the sun. He beamed when he smiled. He was truly special, with a heart bigger than the wooden gazebo.

His summer routine included going to the post office each day and then, after looking both ways, crossing the street to the park. There he would sit on the gazebo steps while he ate his bologna sandwich. It was his favorite place to sit and the birds and squirrels knew it. They didn't care if he wasn't so smart. They didn't even care that sometimes he ate all of his sandwich and forgot to save them some. They just felt something when he laughed that made them feel the same as when they came out of the shadows into the sun on a cold day.

After eating he would tell them his best thoughts, then pull his transistor radio out of his overalls, place it next to his ear, and dance around the smooth wooden floor of the gazebo. He loved music and movement. Evoli was a strange sight, all right, as he danced with his imaginary partner. Later in the day, his grandmother would walk over from her part-time job at the courthouse to take him home with her. That was how his summer passed.

The night of the Autumn dance was gorgeous. Evoli

stood on the post office steps and listened as the band-master began to auction off dances with the Peach Queen and her court. It was a tradition, and the money raised went to the local library. Evoli had always done as his grandma had instructed, but this night he felt such an urge to dance that he looked both ways, then crossed the street to the park. Later, he'd tell his grandma that he had disobeyed her instructions to watch the dance from the steps of the post office. But for now, Evoli wanted to be inside the music box.

The girls were beautiful. The music was beautiful. Evoli was beautiful. Evoli even had three crumpled dollars in his overalls. He was rich.

"How much is the opening bid for a dance with this beautiful lady of the Queen's court?" the bandmaster asked.

"T'ree dollars," came the voice of Evoli Jones from out of the crowd.

"Ten dollars," said another man.

"Twenty dollars," said another.

"Anymore bids?" asked the bandmaster. "Going, going, gone. Sold to the man in the blue suit for twenty dollars," the bandmaster replied.

This went on until all ten dances with the young women in the Queen's court had been auctioned off. Each time Evoli had cried out "T'ree dollars," but that was all that he could bid. Each time the crowd had looked at him.

The dance with the Peach Queen was the last to be auctioned. She was the most beautiful lady of them all.

"How much is the opening bid?" asked the bandmaster.

"T'ree dollars," yelled Evoli.

One by one the members of the crowd had slowly come to some marvelous collective insight. The threads of human kindness had woven the crowd together around Evoli. The crowd's eyes were on Evoli as he yelled again, "T'ree dollars."

Their smiles said everything and their voices said nothing. There were no other bids. Just silence and smiles.

"Going, going, gone. This dance is sold to the young man in the overalls for three dollars," the bandmaster said.

Evoli came up the steps of the gazebo. The band played. He danced with the most beautiful girl in the county. It was a special night for a special person. He moved like Fred Astaire, and the way his face glowed the globe lights weren't necessary.

That was the night that certain attitudes were auctioned off in the echoes of "going, going, gone." That was also the night the statues moved.

Fathers Are Mainly Mortal

All fathers dance with
their demons; all sons just can't
hear the music until they too
grow older, then their
own dance begins.
Often, understanding cuts in.

Unknown

At first I thought he was the wisest, wittiest, strongest, smartest and tallest person that ever lived. He was my hero and I hung on his every word, for I believed he knew everything about everything. He seemed to be the bravest person I knew, and when I was with him I felt safe from harm. Then I became a teenager.

Something happened; I'm not sure what, but I began to see my father differently. He really wasn't the tallest or strongest or smartest person, and he often seemed stumped when it came to having all the answers. He was still on a pedestal, but life was eroding the base of this magnificent statue that I thought was at least equal to the statue of Abraham Lincoln.

I don't remember the day his shoulders started drooping when he walked or when he got that faraway look in his eyes. He spent more and more time in the world of his mind and, though we'd still talk, we weren't connected anymore.

His troubled thoughts put him in a trance and he changed in terrifying ways. Too much drinking, too many women, too little understanding and finally, too late, a divorce. Then I became a young man.

He didn't see me get married, but he became a grandfather anyway. He and I grew apart as the children grew up calling him "Granddaddy Longlegs." We had an uneasy truce that always got broken about the same time as the seal on the whiskey bottle. It would be years before I realized he was an alcoholic.

I saw him in the hospital before he died and we talked briefly. There were no words powerful enough to pull our broken relationship back together again. Blood may be thicker than water, but broken hearts just can't pump hard enough to sustain a terminal relationship.

It rained the day of his funeral, but I didn't get wet—I wasn't there. Then I became middle-aged.

Life dealt me many of the cards that my father had held. I'm not too sure I've played my hand any better than he played his. Life has rounded the sharp edges of my idealism, and tolerance gained through understanding allows me to look back with realistic but kinder eyes. I don't think "Ozzie and Harriet" lived in any of the houses in my neighborhood.

The other night I sat in the den and imagined my father sitting there with me. I was the only one home, so I spoke out loud those things I wish I could tell him now.

"Daddy, I sure love you. I wish I had known about alcoholism, so maybe we could have gotten you some help when you first needed it. I wish we had walked and talked more and told each other we loved one another. We should have hugged more and harder and looked into each other's eyes as though each moment was the last moment on earth.

"Daddy, I'm much older now, yet wisdom is still a stranger. I am afraid a lot, but I bet you were too. The more I live, the less I know about life. You, Daddy, were mighty sick with alcoholism, and it took you away from me and me from you."

He stood to go. I never could imagine him sitting still for too long. His demons were always calling him to dance. I got up to say good-bye. In my mind we hugged and our eyes knew each other again. Then he said, "Son, I always loved you. I just couldn't always show it."

So, for my father, and for you other mere mortal fathers out there—which is really the only kind—Happy Father's Day.

A Place at the Table

Certainly, more sons
are prodigals than
prodigies.

Unknown

Thanksgiving Day was a Norman Rockwell painting. Happy relatives were greeting each other in the front yard. Smoke rising from the chimney pointed a wavy finger toward beautiful blue skies with soft, white clouds. Even the autumn leaves lied with their magnificent colors reflecting the sun, dazzling and distracting their admirers from the truth of their impending demise.

It was a scene suitable for framing except that one person was absent from the picture. He had last posed for the Thanksgiving Day picture three years ago, but since then had been whited out with cocaine powder.

He stood in the park across from his parents' home, leaning against the huge oak tree just as he had when he was a kid and was tired from too much play. He was tired now, but it had been a long time since he had played. He stood hidden in the tree's shadow, which shielded him from the eyes of the Thanksgiving travelers arriving at his home.

The thin, young man had been away for three years. He wasn't sure why he had returned. Perhaps it was the magnetic pull of memories of a simpler time that had drawn him home. Maybe he was trying to find some meaning in the lost roots of childhood.

All he knew was that the last years had been tumbleweed times spent drifting from one place to another. His brand of freedom came from the old song about Bobby McGee where "freedom's just another word for nothing left to lose." Cocaine had taken his freedom and his family.

He had gone through one family and two treatment centers, but even a practicing drug addict like Jim remembered the story of how the prodigal son came home. He was the distance of one tree-lined street away. He sat down.

His thoughts went back to his last Thanksgiving at home. His family was big on tradition. His father always sat at the head of the dining room table and, after saying grace, rose and carved the turkey. His mother would always stay up late the night before preparing wonderful side dishes and desserts.

Jim's younger brother and sister would set the table and clean the house, while Jim would rake the yard and clean up outside. Everything was made ready for the yearly company of aunts, uncles, cousins and grandparents. It was a house where living, loving and learning were fostered.

After the food, came football on TV and more snacking and stuffing. Everything was predictable, even the family football game in the park in the late afternoon. That was before cocaine. After cocaine, nothing was predictable except the daily hunt for more white powder at any price.

The afternoon grew older and the ground became cold and damp. Despite all of his parents' pain, Jim knew they would still allow him to come for food and rest. Even the black sheep hears the beckoning cry of the flock.

He really missed his parents, especially his father. Jim couldn't remember the day the twinkle had faded from his father's eyes, but he remembered his father's lifeless stare when he found out Jim had returned to cocaine.

Jim was starving. He had been off cocaine for almost two full days and his desire for food was returning. His hands were shoved deep in his jacket pockets. His left hand gripped the felt lining of his pocket while the right hand closed around the cellophane package of cocaine. He looked across the street when he heard the front door slam.

In the twilight he saw his father standing on the front porch. His father looked up and down the street in a slow, steady, searching manner. Jim saw his father's head suddenly stop, his gaze squarely on the park. He was intently looking for something. Jim flattened his back against the tree. He expected his father to whistle for him to come to eat as he had when Jim was little. His ears strained to pick up any sound. He heard nothing but his breath as his father went back inside the house.

Jim felt colder and emptier. He pulled his collar up and the cellophane pouch out. He held the plastic up close to his eyes. One gram of cocaine can weigh more than an entire family. His hand reached for the zip-lock opening, but the slam of the door froze him.

Through the plastic bag he saw the distorted view of his father returning to the porch with his jacket on. His father stood with his arms folded across his chest. Jim had seen that parental pose thousands of times when his father was upset.

Then he heard it. It was low at first, like the sound of wind through the trees, then it grew louder. It rode on the wind and echoed through the park. It was his father's whistle. He always whistled for him when it was getting dark.

His father unfolded his arms as he left the porch and began walking toward the park. They were spread wide by the time he neared the street.

Jim quickly got to his feet and the cocaine spilled to the ground. He started to run, but his feet were riveted by his father's voice.

"Welcome home, Son, your mother's preparing a place for you at the table. You've played long enough—it's time to come in from the dark."

His father's voice had laid the bridge of reconciliation at Jim's feet. Even a prodigal son can't burn his father's bridge behind him. Fathers' bridges are made of steel, and this one was clear for crossing.

It was dusk and the automatic street lights came on to cast their light upon a father and a son hugging and crying in the street. Mr. Rockwell would have approved.

The Boy
in the Mirror

Acting your age is
often just that.

Unknown

A while back, I saw a small boy standing at a school bus stop. It was a cold morning, and he was bundled up with so many winter clothes that his arms stood out from his sides. As I drove by him, I got a good look at his face. He seemed to be a first-grader.

He looked determined with tight lips and slightly jutting jaw, but his eyes had that wide look of fear. Soon the bus would pick him up and take him off to school. I glanced into my rear-view mirror for one final look at the little boy who I thought resembled nothing so much as a padded penguin. He seemed both powerful and petrified. I drove on toward work. I remembered.

Scared. First day of school. Leaving home to learn. Riding the school bus for the first time, wondering how I would ever get back home. Clutching my Roy Rogers metal lunch box. Immediately falling in love with Mrs. Zuber, my first-grade teacher, whose gentle ways eased my self-doubts.

They say the sense of smell carries the oldest memories. I remembered the smells of first grade just like they were yesterday.

In my mind rose the eternal smells of crayons, rubber erasers, glue, chalk, ink, pages in a new reader and that red sawdust stuff the janitor used to sprinkle on the wooden floors to clean them. I drove on, really happy that the flood of four decades of life experiences had not drowned those first-grade memories.

Remembering when reading *See Spot Run* made me feel like I was just about the smartest person in the whole world.

Remembering growing up in the sweet fantasies of the 1950s where Camelot was somewhere just around the corner. Really believing that the adults had their acts together and surely had all the answers.

Learning the simplified formula for becoming a man in the 1950s: 1) get tough, 2) get drunk, 3) get women, though not necessarily in that order. Gosh, it sure seemed simple enough, but the big people somehow confused me. There were too many things I couldn't understand.

Never quite understanding the difference between being proud of myself and "getting too big for my britches." Never finding the dividing line between being nice to people and "letting people run over me." Never firmly grasping the idea of being respectful to my elders but rude to adult strangers who might lure me off to never-never land with a bag of candy. Never really sure how I could grow up to be a young man if I could "never get too big for a spanking." Really couldn't understand getting severe spankings for not fighting, and then getting severe spankings for fighting.

I was supposed to treat everyone the same, with the exception of anybody who was of a different race, color, religion or neighborhood. I even learned super myths such as "real men don't cry," "real men can hold their booze," and "real men are never afraid." It seemed the messages of the 1950s left me dangling somewhere between the concepts of a mass murderer and a mama's boy. I drove on.

I suppose my childish days are over, aren't yours? I've got it all together now, don't you? I must admit though, there are some days I practice positive thinking, and other days I'm not positive I am thinking.

Nowadays, I see young people and realize I have become part of the adult conspiracy to make them think we grown-ups really know what we're doing and what's best for them. And of course we do, don't we?

I finally pulled into the parking lot at work. As I was getting out of the truck, I glanced into the rear-view mirror. There I saw a little boy with gray hair and a grin. He looked a lot like the first-grader I had passed on my way to work—both powerful and petrified. Some things never change, I thought, as I shut the door. In retrospect I imagine the silliest question of the 1950s must have been, "When are you going to grow up?"

Easy Writer

They say you can't
outrun the Grim Reaper; yet,
a Harley gives you hope
for a little while.

A Middle-Aged Motorcycle Guy

Why in the world would any sane adult want to learn to ride a motorcycle? They are dangerous vehicles, to which most parents and physicians will readily attest. Best to stick with an automobile, maybe one of those with steel reinforced doors, found mainly in the parking lots of Volvo dealers and private schools at pickup time. That's the way to go alright. At least he felt that way until last November. That was when he fell victim to the vicissitudes of the proverbial middle-age crisis. Why, at his age he should have been thinking more like someone in the middle ages. But he wasn't. When your father is dead and you are older than your doctor, you sometimes wander off into foul territory.

Lust is such a lowly trait. So, each day, as he drove by a local motorcycle dealer's business on the way home from work, he would only cast a sideways glance at the motorcycles gleaming through the showroom window. Then it happened. One night, in a fit of brazen disregard for his station (wagon) in life, he pulled right up to the showroom window and furtively got out. Pressing his face against the window to cut the glare, he gazed over the beautiful machines like some lovesick sheik in his harem. Sure, they were foreign bikes, but then any bike was foreign to him at the time.

He hadn't stood at the window long before he started to hear voices in his head. He heard his parents' voices warning him about the dangers of having a motorcycle. Then he heard his colleagues' collective chuckle. He even had visions of a motorcycle gang looting and pillaging quaint little southern towns as southern belles with a minimum of three names cowered outside the cotillion.

He quickly turned up his coat collar to hide from the eyes of passing motorists. He couldn't have felt any more paranoid if he had been standing in front of a porno movie theater. He slunk back to his station wagon. "I'm a lucky man," he thought to himself, "I own a wagon."

Well, that was the fateful night the obsession began to grow. He had not ridden a motorcycle in over 20 years, and that one was just a trail bike. Could he ride it? A street bike of all things! Why not? Act your age! No fool like an old fool! What would the neighbors say? He remembered a line from Seneca: "Those afraid of dying are afraid of living." Then it suddenly came to him that he was old enough now that no one would tell him no. After all, he was closing in on 50 faster than a poor man facing a pile of pancakes.

He just wasn't destined to become a normal middle-aged guy. If he had been he would have bought a bright red convertible, a bad toupee, found himself a woman who had no idea who Bing Crosby was, and purchased three pairs of full-figured denims that might delude him into thinking his rear end didn't resemble a Peruvian mountain range.

Two weeks later he bought the motorcycle. It took a while, but he learned to ride it. Twice he dropped it at low speed, but there was no serious damage except to his ego. He thought 40 miles per hour was really flying, and he just knew he would never feel confident enough to get out on the dreaded interstate with all those trucks. Two weeks later he passed a tanker truck on the inter-state and laughed heartily. He was learning to ride and he loved it. Still, he was merely a jockey on a steel steed, and he soon found out that most motorcyclists are more than mere jockeys. They are more like veterinarians who know what's on the inside of their charges. He had a lot to learn.

He rode 2,000 miles in November. It was cold outside, but he continued to feel warm inside. In January, he traded up for the largest used motorcycle in the showroom. It was still new to him and it was beautiful. Only a handful of people still thought commitment procedures should be sought, but mothers are tenacious that way.

Well, 15,000 miles have gone by since then, and he waxes eloquent when he talks about how numb his hands get riding in the dead of winter. He rode to the 50th anniversary of Bike Week in Daytona, Florida. He can tell you what 50 mile per hour gusts of wind will do to a motorcycle, and how much you have to lean in order to stay upright. He was among the 600,000 motorcyclists that roared in that week, and a good many of them continued to list to the right as they walked. Being on a foreign bike instead of a Harley, he still felt like an outsider. He was James Stewart at a James Dean convention.

Nevertheless, he says he has met some interesting people who are motorcyclists. For instance, there was a group of Vietnam veterans from Texas who had small American flags on their vests with the words, "Try to burn this one and see what happens." Talking with them would do nothing but burn a hole in your heart, for these were gallant men who deserved far better than they had received.

He met a bearded mountain man from Tennessee with a rattlesnake rattle earring. The inscription written on the chrome of his bike read, "Is there life after death? Touch this bike and find out." He got full permission before he even looked at this guy's bike any further, and even then it was from across the street in the event he needed a head start.

He met a very tough biker with tons of tattoos and a T-shirt which told people he loved them. Well, it didn't exactly say "love," but it did have a "you" on it. He couldn't have been too evil, though, because he had his tiny dog securely strapped in the special rider's seat behind him.

He says he likes most bikers because they don't have too many cards up their sleeves. What you see is what you get. They like to live and let live, and really just want to have fun, with the exception of those rare few who have a devilish desire to carve a road map of New Hampshire on your face.

He says riding at night under the stars is as close to flying as a human can possibly come. It's as though you have wings. To ride on a sunny day is beyond all description, he says.

Even though this guy allegedly has a Ph.D., you can tell he isn't very smart. In fact, he himself says he needed to get another Ph.D., and he did . . . a PRETTY HARLEY-DAVIDSON.

A Morning of Motivation

Shame on the soul, to falter on
the road of life while the
body still perseveres.

Marcus Aurelius

It was the kind of day I hoped God would Xerox and tomorrow return its duplicate. It was early morning, but the sky had already finished painting itself with a fresh coat of bright blue. The air was crisp with each breath, and it smelled fresh and fragrant.

The day was as invigorating as entering the old neighborhood drugstore in the summer when I was a kid; the drugstore was one of the few places that had air conditioning. Dogs felt brand-new and pranced with their owners around yards and school bus stops as though gravity had been called off for the day.

Weather affects a person's mood, and this day beautifully deluded me into thinking all was right with the universe. I was on my way to work in a wonderful world. The windows were down and my spirits were up.

My '72 Pinto with its green Rustoleum paint was a constant reminder that I hadn't been out of the university very long. I wasn't as eccentric as I was broke, but my "unmarked garbage truck" was running just fine as I pulled in behind the yellow school bus.

The children on the school bus were in high spirits too. They were laughing and pointing in my direction. I thought they were amused by my pitiful Pinto, so I laughed and waved back at them. They were still laughing and pointing as the school bus pulled away. Only then did I realize they weren't directing their laughter at me. Out of the corner of my eye I saw a child rushing to catch the school bus; I turned to see her hurrying up the sidewalk as she came even with my car.

The contrast between the beautiful day and what I saw made the impression that much more powerful. The sight of that little girl branded my brain and seared my senses.

She evidently had just come out of one of the houses that lined the narrow street. She had braces on her arms and legs, and her schoolbooks were strapped to one of her arms. She struggled and lurched along as fast as she could, but in her heroic haste the books broke loose and tumbled to the sidewalk. Still, she wouldn't quit, and she awkwardly bent down in a vain attempt to gather the books back up.

Even while she was making frantic, uncoordinated efforts to pick up the books, she never took her eyes off the school bus, which was now almost a block away. Still, she wouldn't give up, and I saw her little face twisted in pain and fear as she yelled with a broken voice, "Wait. Wait. Wait for me."

A woman came hurrying down the street toward her. I drove about a block before I had to turn down a side street and stop my car. It was a clear day, but there was rain in my eyes.

It was a long time before I could tell anyone about the events of that day without getting choked up. At first, I wasn't sure why I had been so emotionally moved by what I had seen. It seemed to be the extreme contrast between the gorgeous morning and the grotesqueness of the situation. Later, I thought perhaps it was the stark realization that children could be very cruel due to their ignorance and immaturity—although I was sure they were no more cruel than we adults, although perhaps a little less ignorant. After a while, I understood what the situation had meant.

In our treatment center, we discuss this courageous little girl with patients whenever we tell them about how much motivation they need to get well. I tell them about the time I saw a little girl with more courage in her little finger than I had in my whole body.

I had spent most of my days running away from life till then, and here was a child who was running toward it with every fiber of her handicapped body. Fortunately, she was less handicapped than I.

Waiting

Half the agony of living
is waiting.

Alexander Rose

It was early morning. It was late fall. The park was empty. The man's heart was full. He sat waiting.

The concrete picnic table still held last night's cold. Now it released its chill to the man sitting on one of the bench seats sipping hot coffee. The trees released their leaves. The sun released its warmth. The man released his thoughts . . . and waited.

His mind was a prison. His mind was a palace. Time released two hours. He killed time. Time killed him. Still he waited. Anticipation started aching.

He had kept his word. He hadn't written it down. The heart never forgets its instructions. It was the right table. It was the right date. It was the right hour. One year to the day, they had said. They'd meet at the same place; they had promised.

Pleasure and pain played "chase" in his mind; so did heartache and hope. The words of Charles Dickens finally made sense. "It was the best of times, it was the worst of times . . . it was the spring of hope, it was the winter of despair, we had everything before us, we had nothing before us." His wasn't a grand story like *A Tale of Two Cities*, it was a simple story about two complex people. He and his unfinished story waited together to find out how the ending would be written. He was the paper. The other person was the pen. So he waited.

Lover's vows are often spoken before the priest of passion, only to be renounced later before the rector of reason and reality. They had loved. They had vowed. They had parted. He had returned. He lingered. He looked. Soon, he must leave.

The park became crowded with people. His eyes strained. She was nowhere. Her memory was everywhere. The day suddenly seemed colder. He had wanted to spend a lifetime with her. He had spent what seemed a lifetime sitting at the concrete table.

He was hungry and cold. His stomach's hunger said go. His heart's hunger said stay. The sun began to drop. His fear began to rise. Shadows began to fall on the park and in his soul.

He pulled her last letter from his coat pocket. It was worn thin from constant handling and reading. She had moved, it said. Best not to give him her new address, it said. She needed time, it said. She couldn't write him, it said. She loved him and would meet him in the park as she had promised, it said. He gently folded the relic of their romance and put it safely into his coat pocket.

When he had moved he didn't leave a forwarding address either. Since she didn't write him anymore, he didn't think it was important. They were two ships in the night. The park was their port. One year was a long voyage for their vows to make. He had faith. He waited.

He closed his heart right after they closed the park. He stood beside the locked entrance gate. He called himself a fool. He locked the door to his heart. He opened the trap door of cynicism. He said he would never love again. He wrote "the end" on the paper in his mind. He even rewrote the romance story so that everything about it seemed ugly. The church of cynicism had a new convert that night. He walked into the dark.

The concrete picnic table was stone cold again, and it was pitch black when her car pulled up to the locked park gate. Her calendar watch had said the 31st. She loved the watch. He had given it to her. She knew the meeting in the park was to be on the first day of

December. She couldn't believe it when she heard the man on the evening news say it was the first of December.

She called herself a fool. "Thirty days hath September, April, June and November . . ." she had yelled over and over again as she drove hurriedly toward the park. She had failed to reset her watch.

She knew she was too late. She would have written a happy ending with permanent ink. The pen was there. The paper was gone. Slowly she put her car in reverse.

As she backed into the street her headlights swept across the statue of John Whittier, which stood near the park entrance. She didn't bother to read the words engraved on the marble plaque beneath it which read, "Of all sad words of tongue or pen, the saddest are these, 'It might have been.'"

No woman reads such lovely words engraved in stone, especially when her headlights are shining upon her lover sitting in solitude at the foot of the statue.

The Mourning After

Older men declare war.
But it is youth that must
fight and die.

Herbert Hoover
Republican National Convention
Chicago, Illinois
June 27, 1944

It was early in the morning on July 5th. Dew blanketed the grass of the small town cemetery, except where footprints led up to a grave with a flat headstone. A middle-aged woman dressed in a plain housedress stood there in silence holding a baby.

Main Street ran back down the hill away from the cemetery. Just yesterday there had been a big parade there. Now the street was cluttered with trash and the spent paper bodies of burned out fireworks. Soon the street sweepers would be at work, and when they were finished it would be as though the parade had been somewhere in a dream. The woman wished she had been somewhere in a dream. But recently everything was too real.

Yesterday, the celebration committee had asked her to sit on the platform where the local politicians would come to praise the war efforts of the townspeople. She refused. She figured nobody gave her special praise like that for raising her son, and she sure wasn't going to accept special recognition now that he'd been killed in the Gulf War. The committee said she wasn't being patriotic, that all they wanted was to honor her son by presenting her with a plaque. She told them she didn't need a plaque to honor or remember him. She said nothing else as she walked away. Now her legs seemed too weak to walk as she stood over his grave.

"Good mornin', Mrs. Smith," came the voice of Jeremiah, the caretaker for the cemetery. He stood reverently at a distance with his old hat in his hand as he waited for Mrs. Smith to answer. She said nothing. He tried again.

"That sure is a fine looking baby, Mrs. Smith. Ain't that your son's baby?"

Mrs. Smith sighed, then signaled with her free hand for him to come closer. "Good morning, Jeremiah. I haven't seen you since Bobby's funeral. It's good to see you."

He spoke as he strolled toward her. "I'm mighty sorry about young Bobby, Mrs. Smith. I reckon you done had a powerful lot of hurt in your heart. Is there anything I can do?"

She hesitated for a moment, then said, "Jeremiah would you please hold the baby a minute for me? I feel sort of tired."

"Yes, Ma'am," he said as she placed the baby in his giant hands. She knelt to rest for a moment. Then, as though her hands had to be busy, she began to rearrange the flowers.

"You know, Jeremiah," she said as she gently spread the flowers, "my husband Robert died in Vietnam, and now Bobby is gone too. Now they're side by side. Both were men who never got to know their sons. What was it all for? Tell me, Jeremiah, what does it all mean?"

Jeremiah stood at attention like a schoolchild being quizzed. He thought for a moment then said softly, "I don't rightly know, Mrs. Smith. I don't rightly know."

She placed the last flowers, then rose to her feet. Something seemed to rise inside her that had become too difficult to hold back. "Jeremiah, my mind is full of awful thoughts lately. Sometimes I feel I must be going plumb crazy." Her voice was quivering.

"What is it Mrs. Smith?" he answered. "You can tell me. Whatever it is, you can tell me and I won't tell no one. You got to let what's burdening you be set free." He held the baby tightly.

Mrs. Smith began to talk. "I've been thinking a lot of

things aren't right, but I'm afraid to tell anybody. I've been afraid to speak out. Do you understand, Jeremiah?"

Jeremiah nodded. "Yes, Ma'am, I sure do," he said.

"Jeremiah, do you know what the word opportunistic means?" she asked with raised eyebrows.

"No, Ma'am, Mrs. Smith. I sure don't. What does it mean?" he asked.

"Opportunistic means taking advantage of the situation, usually a bad one, without regard to basic principles." She continued. "I think this war was nothing but a case of opportunism and a political maneuver to build up the president's popularity. He knew we were going to win or he wouldn't have taken the chance of entering into the war."

Jeremiah patted the baby, "Sort of like a fixed heavy-weight fight, huh?"

"That's right," she stuttered, "and I resent that a lot of industries got rich off the war. All those arms dealers, all those flag makers and T-shirt companies, the ribbon manufacturers, and even all those contractors making millions to rebuild Kuwait."

Jeremiah couldn't answer. He just stood there.

"And another thing," she said angrily, "that big shot general is getting five million dollars to write his life's story. I don't think a man should get rich for getting people killed. If he was such a genius, why is my son dead? Who's going to raise my grandson? I miss my son. I'm tired of my men dying in vain. Nothing changed in Vietnam and nothing's going to change in Iraq." She was shaking and crying angry tears.

Jeremiah handed her the baby in hopes she would calm down. She took the baby, then said, "Jeremiah, this boy will never die in a war. Do you hear me? This boy will never die in a war!"

"Yes, Ma'am," he said, "I believe you!"

She said her good-byes to him and started her long walk back home.

Jeremiah thought how much he would have loved to have taken her to the drug store for a soda, but he knew how the local folks felt about that kind of thing.

Freud Will Be Back
in February

The unexamined life is
not worth living.

Socrates

The overexamined life leaves
no time for living.

Unknown

It was Saturday. It was Atlanta. It was boredom. It was the second day of a three-day seminar on "Violence in American Sports," and the biblical admonition that if time were not short none of us would be saved had started to make a lot of sense.

Thinking the seminar might address the use of cocaine in sports, I had brought an optimistic October attitude and a dilapidated Samsonite suitcase full of perfunctory professional attire comprised of herringbone coat, Hush Puppies, horn-rimmed glasses and a fresh copy of *How to Dress for Success*. I should have known the airport incident was an omen of things to come.

You see, I own a low self-esteem suitcase with more scars than a three-legged dog who loves to chase cars. I had been standing at the baggage carousel at the airport pretending I was waiting for someone in order to give the other travelers time to get their bags and clear out. This way, I figured, I could be saved the embarrassment of claiming my battered bag.

The carousel had gone around more times than a finicky dog looking for a place to lie down, and was almost empty when I decided to make my move. About that time the baggage man grabbed my suitcase, held it up like a drowned rat, and yelled, "Did someone forget their luggage?"

Travelers turned around and I turned red, grabbed my suitcase and hurried out of the Atlanta airport faster than that football guy heading for a rental car.

It seemed somewhat appropriate that the seminar was

being held in a convention center located in a high crime area of the city where the cry "tank" instead of "taxi" would have been more realistic, and I'm not sure the cost of the seminar wasn't a new form of something called "way high robbery."

To be blunt, the seminar stunk. Had Mr. Nobel been alive, he would have been throwing dynamite toward the podium rather than awarding prizes.

The presenters first gave us a complete copy of their professional papers, then stood at the podium and read aloud the very same paper they had handed out. Some sort of advanced "see Freud run" technique, I suppose.

The afternoon consisted of breaking up into discussion groups to rehash the morning presentations, playing about one hour of one-upmanship, and pretending our pontifications really made sense. The presenter was droning on, my attention span was fading fast, and my mind began to wander back to my days at the University of Alabama. Now there were some days of social significance.

Watching fall football practice and Coach Bryant, the growling god of gridiron, climbing up into the tower. Whistles and contact and everybody praying they were doing well enough to keep Coach Bryant from coming down from the tower. Never hearing any of the assistant coaches foolish enough to call him "Bear."

Football season on the way. Crisp days and camaraderie. Coeds and corny football jokes. Booze and binoculars. Pimples and pomp. Homecoming, that special event when the prodigal sons come home to watch the members of the vicious visiting team method act their roles of lemmings and dash headlong to be drowned in defeat to the delight and delirium of the home crowd.

Saturday morning stories about the "Galloping Ghost" and the "Bear" being told by friendly liars resting in lawn chairs on the cement. Game day and a parking lot full of vans, Winnebagos and a relatively new species called "tailgaters" turning the parking lot and weekend into a concrete carnival of crowds, color and enough Coors-induced camaraderie and confusion that I half-expected to hear the voice of Marlin Perkins murmuring, "Jim will try to get closer."

Alumni with old faces and young feet filing into the stadium as game time nears. Coeds in chic clothes practicing perfect reciprocity: traveling up and down the stadium stairs as stadium stares travel up and down the coeds. Math professors having trouble locating their seat numbers, engineering professors raving on about the advanced circuitry in the new electronic scoreboard, cheerleaders yelling their pun, "two bytes, four bytes . . ." Accountants wearing ascots and discussing mascots, and the great pageantry flows on and the day seems perfect. The national anthem and Old Glory being raised on the flagpole. Everybody standing up for the kickoff.

For several hours the tides of emotion rush violently and crash on the retainer walls of the stadium, and for a brief period of time the lives of "quiet desperation" are forgotten in the drenching spray of sensation and excitement of the game.

It was after lunch, we were in the discussion group, and I heard the woman's voice next to me. "Well, Dr. Eades, do you agree with Dr. Freud's concept that a sport such as football is simply a cathartic mechanism, whereby individuals are able to identify with the aggressors and thereby ventilate their pent-up, aggressive impulses through an acceptable social outlet, and thereby dissipate the antisocial expression of anger and aggression, or do you agree with Dr. Bandura that football is negative, in that the behavior serves as a model of rewarded violence which will be emulated by those observing the actions which are condoned by the crowd?"

I glanced at my Timex and wondered if the advertisement, "It takes a licking and keeps on ticking," could be considered violent. You see, I was checking to see if I could make it back to the hotel in time to watch the football game on television.

The woman continued, "You seem to be resistive, Dr. Eades. I see you looking at your watch, which I construe as a passive-aggressive maneuver to avoid active participation in this discussion group. Aren't you interested in this vital issue?"

I leaned over and whispered in her ear so as not to embarrass her. "As Rhett would say: Frankly, my dear, I don't give a damn." I left the group, feeling free at last, and I knew that if I hurried I could just about make kickoff.

Football or Freud? Get serious. Everyone knows that everything has its own season, and thank goodness, it's football season. I believe that Freud's season starts sometime in February.

The Wall

The only sane response to an
insane world is insanity.

Unknown

I t was Sunday afternoon and the conversation was harder than the concrete bench on which the two men were sitting. Sometimes when talking to a stranger, the words get strangled before they're born, and even small talk can loom large, especially when two people prefer being private to being polite.

So they sat, mostly in silence. Both men would rather have been somewhere else, but all of the other tables were occupied, and the high concrete wall which surrounded them served to keep them captives in the small outside courtyard.

They were prisoners of privacy, but this wasn't unexpected since they were in a state mental institution—or, as the local folks sometimes called it, "the loony bin." Finally, the older man led the escape as his words sawed through the bars of silence.

"Why are you here?" he asked in an overly soft and courteous manner. The young man with old eyes turned slowly like a mechanized mannequin until he made contact with the older man. Then he spoke. "I couldn't be what people expected me to be."

"I don't understand," the older man replied. "What do you mean?"

"I mean," said the young man, "my father wanted me to be a brilliant student so he could brag about me, but then he became ashamed of me for making average grades. He'd rather call me lazy than admit I was average. He couldn't accept his son being like the majority of people. Do you understand?"

"Not really," came the honest reply, as the older man shook his balding head.

"I just couldn't be what he wanted me to be," the younger man went on. "I remember the day he took me hunting. His friends were with him and he made me shoot this beautiful deer to prove to his friends that I was a real man."

"How many points?" asked the older man, evidently a hunter himself.

"None," the young man responded to the obvious question about the antlers. "The whole ordeal was pointless. I cried and he never took me again."

The old man fell silent as the young man continued in a monotone voice.

"So my father wanted me to be an attorney like him, but my mother said I should be a banker like Uncle George. Granddaddy said he wished he could persuade me to be a carpenter like him, and Grandma wanted me to be a minister. My minister thought I should become perfect like God, and my peers pushed me to be a rebel like James Dean."

The older man wanted to look away, but found himself mesmerized by the young man's eyes. So he listened as the young man continued.

"My girlfriend expected me to be everything, while her father wanted me to be nothing so he could be something. Television told me to use alcohol, cars and women, and the evening news warned me about alcoholism, accidents and AIDS."

The mechanized mannequin stopped suddenly as though he had been unplugged. Then in a stammering voice he said, "I'm sorry, I get a little confused sometimes. Please forgive me. I've been here over a year, and I think I'm starting to find out who I am and what *I* want to be. I don't want to be crazy. How long have you been a patient here?"

The old man's face turned red. "I'm not a patient," came his quick reply. "My nephew has been committed here for several months and I'm just visiting. Do you understand?"

The young man nodded his head knowingly. His eyes grew bright. "Sure, I understand," he said. "You live in that loony bin on the other side of the wall."

What Day Is Halloween?

Outside show is a poor substitute for inner worth.

Aesop's Fables
"The Fox and the Mask"

I t was almost closing time when I entered Hank's Costume and Novelty Shop to buy a Halloween mask.

"How's business, Hank?" I asked as he shuffled around from behind the counter to wait on me.

"It's so good it's frightening," he answered straight-faced before he began that weird laugh of his. It sounded like a possessed piano player practicing the scales; he began on a high note and rapidly went down several octaves. Hank was a character straight out of central casting. His inch-thick glasses magnified his eyes to the size of half dollars. His hooked nose and the huge hump on his back gave him a permanent half-turtle look, as though any moment his head would snap back into his shoulder shell if you approached him too quickly.

"What kind of mask you looking for this Halloween, Doc?" he asked.

"Something really scary, Hank," I said as my eyes roamed over the masks hanging on the wall. "That Frankenstein mask was a big hit at last year's Halloween party."

"You're in luck, Doc. I got some really scary masks this year," he replied, his giant eyes gazing past the wall where the masks hung toward the front of the store. "Forget these masks—they're nothing but child's play. They're just your usual run of the mill monsters— Frankensteins, werewolves, mummies and stuff like that. Every place carries those."

He nodded toward the door in the back of the shop.

"Come with me, Doc. These out here are kid's stuff. I'm taking you back to the secret adult section. I'll show you some masks that will scare the hell out of you."

He led and I followed, fighting a racing heart and a strong urge to say, "That's okay, I'll just take one of those werewolf masks."

The door creaked. His half-dollars turned and looked into my fear-inspired eyes, which were now themselves the size of quarters. "Guess you can tell I don't show people this room very often," he said. "Most folks just can't take it." He pulled a long string hanging from a small bulb in the ceiling, and the dingy light fell on hundreds of masks hung along the walls.

As my eyes adjusted to the dimness, I could see the features of the lifelike masks around the room. My pulse slowed down. "Hank, these aren't scary masks at all," I said. "They're just masks of regular people. There's nothing scary about any of them."

"Better look closer, Doc," he said, cutting loose again with that weird laugh. "You ain't as sharp as I gave you credit for." He walked over and pointed at one of the masks.

"Ever seen this one before?" he queried.

"Well, it sure looks familiar, Hank," I said. "Looks like one of those T.V. evangelists—what's his name?—but what's so scary about that?"

I hesitated. Hank cocked his head. "Don't you think it's scary that a guy like that could con sweet old widows out of their life savings? He didn't pray for vulnerable people; vulnerable people were his prey. I find that terrifying, don't you?"

I paused. "Well, I guess so, Hank. I think I see your point."

He laughed as he put his hairy finger on another mask.

"How about this one? I call it my presidential collage."

"I don't know," I said. "It looks like you've combined the facial features of several presidents I recognize, but I don't feel my blood running cold, if you know what I mean."

"You Ph.D.'s are really dense sometimes," Hank blustered. "It scares me to death to think that leaders of our nation could authorize burglaries, lie to the people and have the Secret Service doubling as pimps. Wake up and smell the coffee, Doc!"

"I guess when you really think about it, it *is* pretty scary," I nodded in agreement. "Hey, I recognize that guy. Wasn't he a trader on Wall Street? I remember now. He ripped-off all the investors who trusted him with their money. That kind of greed is scary."

"By Jove, I think he's got it," Hank mocked.

The more I looked, the more I recognized. Hank was right. These were adult masks, and they were much scarier than the ones in the other room. Hank had become so intense I tried to change the subject.

"Think they'll ever ban Halloween, Hank?"

"Ban Halloween?" he spat. "Why? It's child's play and the masks are off the next day. It's those masks that are worn the other 364 days when no one's suspecting it that scare the willies out of me."

"Well, do you reckon they'll ever stop trick-or-treating?" I asked.

"Wise up, Doc," he answered. "Children don't usually do both. These masks are scary because they are adults who trick to get a treat."

Hank proudly pointed. "This one here is my psychologist's mask, Doc. Pretty scary, huh?"

"Well," I stammered, "I guess it can be plenty scary when people think psychologists have all the answers."

Hank grunted. "Nah, what's really scary is when psychologists *themselves* think they have all the answers."

Hank rubbed his hands together and started a fire in his eyes. "One more, Doc, then we'll go. I'm going to show you the mask of a person who has the potential to be a murderer, a sex fiend and a liar; a person capable of envy, greed, deceit; a person possessing an unlimited ability to be destructive."

Hank had me follow him over to the back wall, then stood back proudly. "Really, really scary isn't it, Doc?" he beamed.

I looked closely. The mask looked absolutely life-like. Mirrors always do that.

The Old Man
and the Tea

The world breaks everyone
and afterward many are strong at
the broken places . . .

Ernest Hemingway
A Farewell to Arms

He was Old Man Wilson. It wasn't a derogatory term, just a reality. He was simply the oldest man any of us knew. He loved animals. He loved people. Mr. Wilson seemed to love everything and everybody, even himself. I was too young to fully appreciate this marvelous creature we called Old Man Wilson, but one day still stands out in my mind

I was a senior in high school and loved to play baseball. Each day after school I'd pass Mr. Wilson's white frame house on my way home from baseball practice. One day he called to me from his front porch, where he always sat in his wooden rocker in the late afternoon.

"Come here, boy," he said, "let me see that baseball glove of yours."

With a few long strides I crossed his postage stamp front yard and handed him my new Rawlings glove with its wonderful odor of brand-new cowhide. There is nothing like the smell of new leather rising up on a spring afternoon, when life itself is fresh with innocence and idealism, and success seems as simple as throwing a fast ball for a strike.

Mr. Wilson slid my glove on his wrinkled hand and pounded his fist into the pocket. "Still needs breaking in," he said more to himself than to me. "Need to put a baseball in the pocket once you've put some glove oil on the leather. Then you tie the glove around the ball with string and let it sit for several days. Best way to do it," he instructed.

"Thank you, Mr. Wilson," I replied politely. "I'll do it

this weekend. Thanks for your help." I was turning to leave when he called me back.

"You'll need a baseball," he said and motioned for me to follow him into his house.

There was a fireplace in his small living room. On the mantel was a baseball sitting on a tiny wooden pedestal. The only other object on the mantel was a tea cup that looked like it had been badly broken and glued back together.

"These are my two prized possessions," he said, smiling as he removed the baseball from its stand. "This baseball was autographed by Babe Ruth one year in Florida, when my wife and I were on vacation and saw the Yankees in spring training. Best player I ever saw," he said. His eyes stared off in the distance as though he might see the Babe there. He placed the ball into my glove. "Okay son, it's yours. Take care of it."

That baseball instantly became my most prized possession, and I must have thanked him a hundred times as I admired the valuable baseball nestled in my glove.

"We have to celebrate this special occasion, boy," he said. "I'll pour us some tea."

Mr. Wilson went into his kitchen, and in a few minutes he returned with a steaming tea pot and one cup. I'd never had anything but iced tea, but I was so grateful I'd have drunk vinegar if he'd have asked me.

"Get my cup off the mantel, boy. We'll go out on the porch."

I carefully removed the tea cup, held it tightly and followed Mr. Wilson through the screened door. An evening breeze greeted us.

I watched him as he poured the tea. He finished, then looked from his tea cup to me, then back to his cup. His eyes beckoned me to ask him, so I did. "Mr. Wilson, I was just curious. Would you please tell me why that tea cup is one of your most prized possessions?" He smiled and cleared his throat, obviously pleased that I was quick to pick up his cue.

"I sure will, boy," he replied as he studied the cup for a moment, then sipped from it. "This tea cup is made of the finest china, and was given to me many years ago by someone I loved. I got mad at that person one night, and hurled accusations at her, and threw this tea cup against the fireplace. It shattered into a thousand pieces. I told her that our relationship was like the remains of this cup, irreparable. Beyond repair. Broken.

"Later that night I came to my senses and looked at all those pieces scattered on the floor. Remembering how much I loved her, I got down on my knees and picked up every piece of that cup. Like a difficult glass puzzle, I started fitting and gluing pieces back together. The cup began to take shape again. It wasn't as beautiful as before, but it was stronger. Finally, several weeks later, I had completely restored the cup. I did it out of love. Guess you might call it my loving cup. Ever since then I always drink from this cup when I have something special to celebrate."

Mr. Wilson raised his cup in a toast, and as our cups met he said, "When things get shattered, sometimes a little patience and the right kind of glue can put them back together again."

The crickets told me it was time to head home. My parents' marriage had recently been shattered by divorce. It would be many years before I was wise enough to understand that my parents just didn't have the right kind of glue.

Better Never Than Late?

You may live a long
while with some people and
be on friendly terms with them
and never speak openly with
them from your soul.

Ivan Turgenev

They had been friends for 17 years. A woman's death had brought them together. It's strange how sometimes a tragedy can fuse a friendship much faster than the passage of time. Bill and Frank, the two fast friends, had finished eating, and now they sat in the corner booth of the restaurant sharing memories of Nancy for dessert.

You see, it was her death that had led to them meeting each other in the first place. Nancy had been Bill's wife, and his life had revolved around her as though she were the sun and he were a planet. In a way, she was really like the sun. She was a bright, beautiful and warm woman who had brought light to Bill's eyes until that tragic day.

On the day of the fatal car wreck, Nancy had been in a hurry. She was driving too fast and, when the tractor-trailer truck in front of her screeched to a halt, she could not stop. It was a horrible thing to see as the twisted metal burst into flames. Frank, who had been in the car behind Nancy, was the first person to reach her car. Driven by adrenaline and fear, he pulled frantically at the collapsed car door, trying to free her.

Frank's efforts were not enough. The fuel from the truck engulfed her car. The truck driver yelled for Frank to get away from the car because it was about to explode, but Frank would not give up. The concussive force of the explosion knocked him unconscious; it tossed him into the air and across the concrete.

Hours later, Frank awoke in a hospital bed to find himself with lacerations, but luckily no broken bones. He also found Bill standing in his room. Bill tearfully thanked him for his bravery, and they both cried as Bill informed him that Nancy was dead.

Bill and Frank attended the funeral together. The local paper had proclaimed Frank a hero. The mayor would later award him a citation for bravery.

They were tough times and Bill needed someone to talk to. Frank seemed genuinely interested, especially about Nancy and what kind of person she had been. They began to spend many hours filled with coffee and conversation.

As time went by, Bill and Frank became almost inseparable. They had dinner twice a week, went to the cemetery each Sunday, played golf and fished whenever they could get together. Fate had indeed formed this friendship.

Bill took a sip of coffee and then spoke, "Well, Frank, I guess we're starting to look like the original odd couple. I'm obsessive and you're the slob of the duo." Bill chuckled as he pointed to Frank's coffee which had spilled over into the saucer.

Frank dipped his napkin into the saucer to soak up the spilled coffee as he chuckled and said, "Just be grateful I don't slurp it from the saucer."

After the brief levity, a long silence settled in. Finally, Bill broke the stillness and said, "Frank, I sure wish you could have met Nancy. You would have loved her."

Frank's 17-year-old secret had become a teenager longing for freedom, and his words spilled over from the cup of his conscience. "I did love her, Bill. I wish I had had the courage to tell you this the first day I saw you in the hospital room."

"What are you talking about?" Bill asked, not sure what Frank was getting at.

"What I'm talking about, Bill," Frank sighed, "is that Nancy and I had been lovers for almost a year before she was killed. Why do you think I asked you so many questions about her? I was grieving for her just like you were at the funeral."

Bill was stunned. "You're not kidding me are you?" he asked with the face of a terminal patient hoping for another diagnosis.

"No, I'm not," Frank said. "I'm so sorry, Bill. You really are the best friend I've ever had. You see, the truth is, I was following Nancy the day of her death. We were on our way . . . ," he stuttered, "we were on our way . . . to a motel. That's why I was behind her. I never was a hero, Bill, I was just trying to save the woman I loved. Please try to forgive me for deceiving you all these years. The guilt has been terrible."

The two men looked at each other with strangers' eyes that finally softened back into the focused gaze of friends.

Bill exhaled deeply. "Thank you, Frank, for telling me. I know it took a lot of courage. I'm the one who feels guilty now. The truth is, I haven't been honest with you either."

Frank looked confused. "What do you mean?" he asked.

"Frank, I knew Nancy was having an affair with someone, but I didn't know who it was," Bill said. "The night before the accident, I confronted her with my suspicions. All she said was that she had been awfully mixed up lately, but was really in love with an engineer at a local plant. She said she was going to leave me to marry him."

Now it was Frank who looked stunned. "I'm not an engineer. You know that Bill." Frank sat dumbfounded.

"Sure. I know," Bill replied. "That's why I never suspected you. But that's not what I have to tell you Frank.

What I have to tell you," Bill paused to get his composure, "is that I was so angry and jealous that I think I went insane. I tampered with the brake lines on her car, but I never meant for her to die. Please believe me Frank. You must believe me. The guilt has been unbearable all these years."

This was one of those times when no more words were needed. Each forgave the other with an understanding look that rendered words useless. In silence they shook hands.

The silence came to an end when the man in the next booth knocked his plate on the floor trying to squeeze out of the booth to leave. He walked up to the cashier. "Why are you leaving so early, Jim?" the peroxide blonde asked. "Usually you close this place up at night."

Jim smiled a thoughtful smile as he picked up his change from the counter. "You know what, sometimes three really is a crowd," he said to her as he adjusted the slide-rule dangling from his belt and started for the door.

The Sawbuck
Stopped Here

We are all wonderful
gifts waiting to be
unwrapped.

Unknown

He had been out of work for almost nine months. Pride and empty pockets had produced a lot of pain and plenty of self-pity. His heart had become just about as hard as the times, and Christmas Eve caught him sitting in his car at the mall with only a tired ten dollar bill that was as worn out as he was.

His worried wife had wanted to come with him. However, ten dollars has a way of making a man feel tiny, especially when he has to buy Christmas gifts for two teenage daughters and a wife. So his pouting pride pushed her concern aside: he told her he would rather be alone. Alone is not good for a recovering alcoholic with a starving ego feeding on self-pity, anger, resentment and giant helpings of hopelessness, helplessness and worthlessness. So he sat, sober and sulking.

He had parked at the far end of the mall parking lot, and his car's isolation matched his mood. He tugged out the ten dollar bill and stared at it. He could buy insulting gifts or enough alcohol to make him rub out raw reality for a while. He remembered the pain of his drinking days, but he felt things couldn't get any worse. Why not drink?

He decided to buy a bottle of vodka. He felt numb to the cold night air as he got out of his car. A man who's out of work often walks with his head down, and this one did too until he entered the mall. He looked up to see bright lights and faces. He saw laughing families and immediately despised them and their moods.

He knew he was doing a lot of "stinking thinking," as they say in AA, but he didn't care anymore. He had lost his attitude of gratitude, and the wisdom of the words "If you can't have what you want, want what you have" had left him.

He walked past the fancy shops and ducked into the liquor store. He ordered a bottle of vodka and put the thin ten dollar bill on the counter. He noticed that someone had written "Mary loves Jack" on the bill. The writing was as faded as his dreams, and he waited impatiently for the man to ring up the vodka.

He left with a bottle-shaped brown bag, 50 cents in change, and as much self-consciousness as an adolescent with a pimple on his nose. He started the long walk toward his car.

As he approached the car, he saw a man in rumpled clothes standing next to it. He could have been a beggar, a bum, a boozer or perhaps all three.

"Hey, Bud," the man said, "can you spare 50 cents for a hot cup of coffee?"

"No, but I'll give you a drink," he replied. "That's what you want anyway, isn't it?"

"Nope, just need money for coffee until I can get back over to the Salvation Army," countered the stranger. "I can't handle the booze. Tried to handle it for 25 years, but it always handled me. In fact, booze cost me my wife and children, my job, my self-respect, everything. Guess you can handle it, huh?"

"No problem here," he said as he lifted the brown bag over his head like a trophy.

"I used to tell my wife Mary that, but I guess the bottom line was that I loved the booze more than anything," sighed the man. "I used to have roots and respect, but now I mostly wander and wonder. Christmas is sort of a bad time for me now. A man ought to have a home to go to on Christmas Eve. I remember one Christmas Eve, we didn't have much of anything, and my wife gave me a ten dollar bill on which she had simply written 'Mary loves Jack.' It was a crisp new ten dollar bill, wrapped up in shiny green paper. She told me to keep it forever to remind me of her love for me, but I wound up getting drunk with it. You know, my wife always said the greatest gift we could give each other was ourselves. She meant listening, loving, time, understanding, humor and all those kinds of things. I never could seem to give myself like that. I could only buy guilt gifts to make up for all the problems my drinking had caused."

The man with the bottle couldn't tell Jack about the ten dollar bill. Besides, he would only think it was some kind of cruel practical joke, and surely there must be more than one ten dollar bill on which someone had written "Mary loves Jack." Instead, he opened the bottle and poured the vodka over the windshield to clear away the frost.

"Sometimes a man can know better how to get home when he is able to see more clearly," he said. He handed the stranger his last 50 cents and smiled, "Merry Christmas, Jack. I've got to hurry home to deliver the greatest gift to my family."

The Kaleidoscope Kid

I gladly would tell you who
I am if only I knew.

Unknown

Monday night on the interstate. Mellow music on the radio. Moments and miles rushing past. Simulating a good Samaritan—giving a semi-stranger, semi-friend a ride home.

I didn't know him very well, although he had often ridden with me. Sometimes, he'd peek out from behind his plastic personality, which featured a smile that stopped too soon to be real. Those were good times: super times—not superficial times.

He could be a poetic person who played with words with as much glee as a child with bright toy blocks. He could build beautiful word pictures, or he could wall you off and hide behind his blocks of big words.

He was a genius and a fool, a saint and a sinner, a friend and a foe. I couldn't tell if he was the guy my grandmother wanted me to grow up to be like or the guy she warned me about. I liked and disliked him. I couldn't figure him out anymore than I could those awful algebra problems in high school. He was the original Kaleidoscope Kid.

I broke our tacit truce of silence to ask, "What are you thinking at this moment?"

"You can't shrink me, Doc. I've been Sanforized," he countered. "Besides, I've got more disguised defenses than the Chicago Bears. Here you are, the quarterback of questions, at the line of scrimmage looking over my defenses, and I suppose you'll be going to an audible any second now. Forget it. Why not just kill the clock? A tie is better than a loss."

"I love football analogies," I said. "Are you a puffed up form of Grantland Rice? Does football build character or characters? Is it really the training ground for life? Bear Bryant, by the way, said a tie was like kissing your sister. Doesn't that sound somewhat incestuous to you?"

He smiled and it didn't fade. "Okay, Doc, I'll give you five minutes of honesty. Just in case your erratic driving brings us to a premature fiery death, at least I'll go out in a blaze of honor and hot metal.

"This moment? I was thinking there must have been millions of moments in my life. Moments, tiny snowflakes of the senses, each a little different, but most melted out of memory. Bright memories, flickering fireflies of thought, ephemeral brightness quickly fading into eternal darkness. Transient thoughts, spending a night in my mind, checking out early, traveling on unemotional expressways to unknown destinations. Too caught up in the dry-lipped demands of day to day reality to stop and smell the roses, as they say.

"Constantly climbing a man-made mountain in my mind, afraid to look back, afraid to look up, looking only for the next crevice to cling to so I won't fall down to my emotional death on the jagged rocks of failure below. Always striving, never arriving. Rushing, not resting. Wearing suits that cost more than my father used to make in a month. I'm a real successful man who's often not real enough to cast a shadow. Some days, I envy the hitch-hiker's freedom, and often have thoughts of gassing up my car and driving off into the sunset. I live the American dream, but have nightmares.

"Moments? Memories? Maybe the question should be, 'have I become a machine?' If I'm the Tin Man, Doc, are you the Wizard? Is this the interstate or the Yellow Brick Road? Have any extra hearts in the trunk, Doc? I'm not like Dorothy; I don't think I'll ever get back home. Maybe Thomas Wolfe was right when he said you can't go home again.

"One last thought, Doc. I read where some guy named Jourard said we live in a world that invites us to die. Isn't that the silliest statement you ever heard?"

I answered none of his questions. They were simply rhetorical, not needing a reply. We drove on in silence. I was relieved when I finally let him out of the car.

I'd never invite him into my house for dinner. Frankly, I wish I never had to let him be a passenger, but often I have no choice.

Sometimes I wonder if this person isn't a secret passenger in many of the cars that travel past me on the highway.

It Ain't Over 'Til It's Over

It is love, not reason, that is
stronger than death.

Thomas Mann

From her window she watched the mailman as he placed the solitary envelope in the mailbox. She waited until he was a respectful distance away before walking briskly down the driveway. Shaking hands, due more to age than anxiety, pulled the lid down.

The early February wind tugged at her fine white hair as she stood before the mailbox and bowed her head to read the envelope. It was a sacred scene, the way she now stood before the metal altar that had saved her from another day of alienation. A faint smile appeared on her wrinkled face. It was good to see Widow Potts smile.

Gripping her precious possession with both hands, she hurried back up the driveway with lighter legs. Seemingly stronger arms opened the kitchen door. She went inside and laid the letter on the kitchen table as though it were an ornate centerpiece. She prepared a cup of coffee, sat down, then ceremoniously slid the paring knife through the top of the envelope. No king bestowing knighthood had ever used a blade more carefully. She pulled the letter from its paper womb with the joy of a brand new mother. She read:

Dear Elizabeth,

As I write this letter to you, I find it difficult to believe that over four decades have passed since last I saw you. I still have the picture of you that you gave me when we were dating in college.

Strange how fate can shape our lives. Had I not been drafted it may have been you and me that got married—instead of you and Herman.

After the service I returned home, but didn't feel it would be appropriate to contact you. I moved out of state the next year.

I still subscribe to the local newspaper and have kept tabs on the town. I read where Herman died last year and I want to extend my deepest sympathy to you. I lost my wife three years ago, and I know your pain has been great, as was mine. The aloneness is excruciating.

I will be in town on business on February 14th and will call you. Maybe we can go out to eat and reminisce.

Sincerely,
William Townsend

P.S. Happy Valentine's Day

A grin spread over her face like butter on a hot roll as she churned up Bill Townsend thoughts from the milk of her memory. My, how she used to love Bill! He was right. Had fate been a little different she would have been his forever. They had been lovers. He had to leave. Loneliness and Herman Potts had done the rest. She had to admit that although she had all the reasons to love Herman Potts, she never had the unreason—that impossible-to-describe feeling where the heart hungers after another human as though heaven or hell is close at hand. Herman was practical. Bill was passionate. Bill . . .

Suddenly Elizabeth Potts felt guilty. Judas in his betrayal couldn't have felt much worse. What would the children say? "Poor Herman would be mortified," she thought, "married to a Jezebel." She hastily put the letter back into the envelope and dropped it into the wastebasket.

Days went by as Widow Potts purged herself of passion's residue. She had made up her mind that she wouldn't give her neighbors any grist for their rumor mills. She didn't want to be the focus of her garden club's gossip, for they were as quick to plant rumors as roses.

More days went by—long gray days that had lost the sun. Elizabeth Potts walked through the mortuary of her mind. Thoughts of tomorrow lay in closed caskets to be mourned only in passing. It was as though her dreams already had been dressed and combed and laid to rest in sterile coffins. But she found no rest, just loneliness.

Nights were the longest. She held her pillows as troubled sleep took forever to come. One night she even thought she heard Herman in the bathroom. She got out of bed with the faith of a Christmas Eve child. But it was just the faucet dripping. "My life is like that faucet," she thought, "Dripping away, little by little." She turned the faucet on full force. "That's the way life should be," she spoke aloud, as the water drenched her nightgown. The cold water made her feel alive and she was grateful for that.

On Valentine's Day the sun found the sky again. The overwhelming beauty made her feel sad. Didn't nature know it was even more beautiful when shared by two? The telephone rang.

Widow Potts wasn't sure what happened next. Her conscience had already convinced her she wouldn't even pick up the telephone, much less talk to William Townsend. The telephone continued to ring, and almost against her will she picked it up. "Oh, yes. Hello Bill. It's so good to hear . . ."

You know how this story ends. If not, well, it wouldn't be any use to try to explain. As Leo Buscaglia says, "Love is life . . . and if you miss love, you miss life." Don't miss it. It is available at fine souls everywhere.

Judgment Day

We thought
because we had power,
we had wisdom.

Stephen Vincent Benet

I t was judgment day. Sure, it wasn't the "final" judgment day, but no one could have convinced Jacob Johnson of that. He sat at the defendant's table looking up at Judge Oliver Stone who, for all intents and purposes, had taken on the characteristics of a supreme being.

The town of Mayville was never going to be the same again. What had started out as a simple commitment case for mental incompetency had become a "tar baby" trial; the national news media had picked up the story, and wouldn't put it down until a final decision was rendered.

That decision was due today. Judge Stone would have to rule either for or against the defendant, Jacob Johnson. The courtroom was crammed full with spectators and reporters. This was the day Judge Stone would have to have the wisdom of Solomon.

Jacob Johnson was a mystery. No one seemed to know where he came from. He just showed up one day in Mayville about three and a half years ago. Old Man Clark, who owned the junk yard, had felt sorry for him. He gave him a part-time job and let him stay in the metal shack behind the junkyard. The whole town knew Jacob but, then again, no one really knew him.

All the witnesses had testified. Nothing was left now but the summations of the attorneys and Judge Stone's ruling. The prosecuting attorney, Mr. Weisel, rose first to present his summation, as Judge Stone rapped his gavel to quiet the courtroom.

"Your honor," Weisel began, "the people have presented a case based on hard facts. The court psychiatrist has testified that Jacob Johnson's I.Q. score places him in the mental retardation range. However, we do not think that alone is enough to justify his commitment to a state mental institution. Therefore, we have presented testimony that leaves no doubt about Mr. Johnson's behavior: it is too erratic for him to function as a responsible member of this community. He is too defective mentally, emotionally and behaviorally to function without presenting a threat to himself and others." Upon hearing this, Jacob began to sob out loud.

Judge Stone rapped his gavel and spoke to the defense table, "Please control your client." The defense attorney patted Jacob's arm and soothed him quiet. "Now let's continue. Where were you, Mr. Weisel?" asked Judge Stone.

Weisel began again. "As I was saying, Your Honor, the testimony shows Mr. Johnson needs to be committed. Testimony from the city street department shows Mr. Johnson stood in front of the mosquito control truck and refused to move. He was incoherently yelling at the city workers that the spray was killing butterflies. He subsequently was arrested for disorderly conduct."

Weisel went on. "The public health officials have testified that Mr. Johnson's shack was an unsanitary health hazard. Upon inspection they found seven dogs and nine cats residing therein. You also heard testimony that he is always picking up stray animals; the number of animals living in his shack will probably increase. You heard Mrs. Wilson and Mrs. Mueller testify that Mr. Johnson has repeatedly trespassed on their property and stolen their prize roses." Judge Stone adjusted his glasses. Weisel was now in full stride.

Weisel continued. "The local hospital administrator has testified that Mr. Johnson has continued to come on the children's cancer ward after numerous warnings to stay out. Mr. Johnson's behavior was loud and boisterous and his singing was disruptive to the unit. Testimony also showed that he brought the stolen flowers on the unit, and littered dirt and leaves on the floor which contaminated the sterility of the unit."

Judge Stone looked over at Jacob, who was nodding in agreement with what Mr. Weisel was saying.

"Your Honor," Weisel said, as he thumbed through his note cards, "the evidence is overwhelming. Trampling the grass at the city park, ignoring the zoo signs and feeding the animals, frightening people by attempting to run up and hug them; and neighbors have testified they saw him crying every evening at sundown." Mr. Weisel hesitated, looked at Judge Stone, then decided to stop. "The prosecution rests it's case," Weisel concluded.

"We all need a little rest," Judge Stone growled, as he called on the defense attorney to present his summation.

The defense attorney rose and said, "We rest our case, Your Honor. We have no summation."

Judge Stone grunted and called a 30 minute recess. Exactly one half hour later he returned to the bench and court was called to order.

Judge Stone cleared his throat. An expectant hush fell on the packed courtroom. "I find this man guilty," he roared. Mr. Weisel allowed a smug smile to cross his face, as big tears rose and fell from the innocent eyes of Jacob. Cameras clicked as the courtroom noise level rose to an unbearable height. Judge Stone furiously pounded his gavel until silence reigned once again. He had something else to say.

"I said I find this man guilty, and he is," the Judge said sternly. "He is guilty of loving too much, of having too much tenderness, of having too much innocence, of having too much caring and of having an overwhelming passion for life."

The courtroom was silent now on its own accord as Judge Stone continued. "Jacob Johnson is guilty of giving a home to abandoned dogs and cats, of bringing stolen flowers to sick children, of crying at the beauty of sunsets, of making joyous noises in a hospital, of feeling the wind from the butterfly's wings on his face, of feeding hungry caged animals, of disturbing lonely strangers with hugs."

Judge Stone asked Jacob Johnson to stand. "As regards the commitment procedure of Jacob Johnson," he said, "I feel we have a case of double jeopardy: this man is already committed." A murmur ran through the courtroom.

Judge Stone continued. "Jacob Johnson is committed to love. In all my years on the bench I think this so-called retarded man's behavior is the closest example I have ever seen to the compassion of Christ. Ladies and gentlemen, I will not be this city's Pontius Pilate. I wash my hands of this matter. I can find no punishable guilt in this man, and I am convinced he is the sanest person within the walls of this courtroom."

Judge Stone rose to his feet. "May God show us the mercy and love this man has shown to our city. This case is dismissed." The gavel rang out.

The Luck of
the Irish

Fortune brings in some boats
that are not steered.

Shakespeare

T he St. Patrick's Day parade had ended many hours before, but he didn't care. He no longer cared for saints, Irish or otherwise, but he cared greatly for Irish whiskey. In fact, it was his love for Irish whiskey that had prompted him to begin his personal parade from bar to bar until now, too drunk to walk, he sat slouched in a dingy corner booth at O'Bryan's Bar and Grill.

He stared into his whiskey glass. The maudlin strains of "Danny Boy" drifted through the smoky room. As he listened to the haunting lyrics, Danny O'Kiley laughed a gallows laugh, imagining himself a tragic bit player in a surrealistic movie directed by a foreign director. "Shakespeare was right," he thought, "Any tragedy carried to its extreme becomes a comedy." His sarcastic laugh was muffled by the shot glass he unsteadily raised to his mouth.

Danny O'Kiley really was a tragic figure. He had become an Irish caricature without the fine character he once exuded. He never intended to become a two-dimensional cartoon character suffering from alcoholism. In truth, he had started out as a good Irish boy who grew into a good Irish man.

Danny O'Kiley's father had died from alcoholism when Danny was 12. Danny vowed at that time that he would never let the same thing happen to him. It was an earnest vow, but spoken in ignorance and with a terrific naivete about alcoholism. His young mind didn't realize that alcoholism wasn't a question of will power. So, as he grew older, he too began to drink Irish whiskey.

Gradually, his inherited tendency for alcoholism began to express itself. Of course he denied it, but the cravings and loss of control were evident, especially to Danny's superiors. Danny was a good man who now had a bad disease. He was sick, not sinful, but he was given a choice by his superiors: get to treatment or get to packing. Danny's sick ego embraced his false pride, and together they helped him refuse to get treatment. Well, that's not such a wise decision when a man is an Irish Catholic priest. He was unfrocked.

He took another drink. "When Irish Eyes are Smiling" mocked him from the juke box. There had been times when his eyes not only smiled, they even laughed lustrously.

Most of those times came when he was a young priest serving a local parish. He had led his parishioners to God as though he were a pied piper priest putting music to all of God's words. That was before the words of Father Martin became a reality: "First the man takes a drink, then the drink takes a drink, then the drink takes the man." He no longer cared to help people find God. He didn't even know where God was anymore. His once tall God now had become very short—no taller than a shot glass. He lifted his glass god to his lips and took another swig.

It was just after dawn when Danny O'Kiley was shaken awake from his drunken sleep. The alley had been his bedroom for the night, and newspapers had been his covers.

"Is that you, Father O'Kiley? Are you alright?" came the words of a woman standing over him.

"Leave me alone," he scowled. The new sun made him squint as he tried to focus on this woman who seemed so tall above him.

She shook him again with more persistence. "Father

O'Kiley, have you been hurt?" she asked.

"No, I've been drunk, you fool," he sneered. "What's wrong with you? Are you so stupid you don't recognize a drunk when you see one? And don't call me Father again, do you hear me?"

Undaunted, the woman continued to shake him. "Get up, stay up, stand tall, it makes you closer to God." She began to pull on his arms and she started to almost chant the words again: "Get up, stay up, stand tall, it makes you closer to God."

The words echoed down the vacant alley and deep into O'Kiley's brain. He had heard those exact words before. Sure he had. He was the one who had spoken them many years before.

"Father O'Kiley," she pleaded, "please get up. I love you, Father O'Kiley," she said as she pulled him up to his feet. O'Kiley searched her face with bloodshot eyes that sought to recognize her.

"It's me, Father O'Kiley. It's Patsy Kelly," she said with true smiling Irish eyes. "Don't you remember me?" He looked at her closely and from somewhere a spark of memory lit his face.

"It's me, Patsy Kelly, remember me? The tallest girl in St. Michael's School," she said.

Patsy went on, "I sure remember you, Father O'Kiley. I could never forget you. You saved my life. Remember how depressed I was about being so tall? I used to slouch down, and once even thought about killing myself. I came to see you at the church to ask you if suicide was the unpardonable sin. I'll always remember what you said, 'Get up, stay up, stand tall, it makes you closer to God.'"

Suddenly, Danny O'Kiley began to cry. Not silent tears but great heaving sobs that shook his body. He howled as the hounds of heaven devoured the devils in his soul.

Patsy's gentle hands led him from the alley to her car parked out on the street. "I'm a nurse at a hospital where they treat alcoholism, Father O'Kiley. I'm taking you there right now. I love you, Father O'Kiley," she said, and she squeezed his arm before placing him in the front seat of her car. He offered no resistance. Who could resist an angel like Patsy Kelly?

Riding to the hospital, Father O'Kiley looked over at Patsy and asked, "Why were you in that alley, Patsy? What were you doing there?"

Patsy said, "I was driving down the street when one of my hubcaps popped off. I saw it roll into the alley. I was looking for it when I found you."

A big grin came over Father O'Kiley's face when he said, "The luck of the Irish, wouldn't you say?" The rising sun caught two pairs of Irish eyes smiling.

New Year's Resolutions

After all is said and done,
all is said and
nothing is done.

Unknown

It was early January. Two hunters were walking beside a country stream, their words of New Year's resolutions strutted before them.

They spoke of how this year definitely would be different, what with all the wonderful changes they were going to make in their lives. This year, without a doubt, they would make those changes they had failed to make last year. They would have done them then, of course, if it hadn't been for all those extenuating circumstances.

Anyway, they agreed, "that was then and this is now." And now they would do those very things that would make them healthier, wealthier, wiser and happier, and would improve the quality of their lives in, well, just about every area. From their words of conviction, their prey, could they understand English, would have thought they were hunting happiness rather than them.

Suddenly, both men stopped as they came upon a strange sight: hanging from a low tree limb was a beautiful bird cage. They went closer for a better look.

A large lock, its metal frown firmly in place through the latch, had the door to the cage securely closed. When they looked into the cage, they saw a dead bird lying to one side. On the other side was a dry, crusted water dish and empty seed husks.

"What do you make of it?" asked the younger hunter.

"Looks like some kind of lovebird to me," replied the older hunter, as he rubbed his hands along the glittering bars of the cage. "It's not very cold, so I imagine the poor thing died of thirst or hunger. I bet you a dollar to a doughnut it belongs to that old hermit the farmer told us about when we got his permission to hunt here."

The younger man pondered for a moment, then spoke. "It sure seems ironic that the bird died right here beside this sparkling stream, and not more than 50 feet from a field full of grain. Don't you think it must have been torture to be so close to what it desired, and yet be unable to obtain it?"

The older man studied the bird carefully, then said, "I don't see any marks on this bird, and there aren't any loose feathers in the cage, so I figure it didn't even struggle to get out. It sure lived in a fine cage while it lived, though."

As he finished talking, they both pulled out some food and sat down to eat.

Each of the men swallowed their sandwiches and thoughts in silence. Some things are too difficult to think, much less voice.

Each of them lived in mighty fine cages, but didn't realize the cost. They had traded risk for routine, romance for reality, chance for comfort, passion for prudence, desire for duty, creativity for company-man, fun for formality and morals for money. Yet they were as unaware of these trade-offs as if they were dead as the bird.

The older man rose and spoke first. "I sure would like to have that beautiful cage, but I imagine it belongs to the hermit and he'll be back to get it. Wonder if he knows the bird is dead?"

"Maybe," said the young man as he stood up and stretched. "Some folks say hermits know nothing, while others say they know too much. What I do know is I'm ready to go and kill my own bird."

The young man walked over to the cage for one final look. Then he saw it. It was something he had missed before when he had looked at the cage. Next to the hook from which the cage was hanging was an opening that had been made by someone who had neatly sawed away several rows of bars. He called to the older man.

"Come look at this. There's a hole in the top of the cage. The bird could have escaped. Guess it was too stupid."

The older man went over and stared at the opening, but couldn't understand how he, himself, could have possibly missed such an obvious way out.

"Well, I'll be damned," he said—and maybe he was.

Sunday Morning
Memories

The soul always cries out for
love. When it is given nothing
but sex—it only cries.

Unknown

Neon, nylons, nightcaps and nakedness. The sin of Saturday night faded slowly into the sun and promised the salvation of Sunday morning. He felt like he did when he came out of a movie during the daytime; when the sun hurts the eyes and the mind is still in a daze from hours in the darkness of projected fantasies. It took a period of time for him to get reoriented to his surroundings. The adjustment took longer this time. Of course it did, he was in a different city.

Different cities never seemed to make a difference. He couldn't seem to run away from himself. If it were possible to escape from himself, he surely would have done it. The floor of his hotel room said he had not changed. Clothes were scattered everywhere. If he were an adolescent, he would surely receive a parental rebuke. But adolescence was just a distant memory for him, even though he still acted like a child. Instead, his parental rebuke came in the form of a calloused conscience. It called to him in a voice hoarse from years of screaming over the noise of self-gratification. It told him it was time to stop this insane behavior. He sat up in bed.

He was able to separate his clothes from those discarded by the woman he had met last night. Intimacy with a stranger isn't much more than a farcical passion play, where the conscience gets crucified and the body is sacrificed as though Heaven is in the offering. Unfortunately, sometimes the conscience can be buried so deep that not even a remnant of remorse can be resurrected. Meanwhile Heaven becomes nothing more than heavy breathing and hearts that would break if they weren't pressed together between the bodies of two people seeking to pull each other inside to fill up that awful emptiness that gnaws with the pains of starvation of the soul.

He dressed in silence this Sunday morning, and prayed a cheap prayer that the woman wouldn't wake before he could leave. Hangovers and half-hearted heartaches always shared the same bed in his brain. He didn't even know her name. To him she wasn't much more than a piece of meat with mascara. He no longer needed the lies he once used to feed his ego. He wasn't a ladies' man and a great lover; he knew the woman wasn't a lady and they surely weren't in love. In truth, he didn't love anyone, including himself.

He shuffled into the hotel coffee shop with all the other convention cattle. It took four cups of coffee, three glasses of water, and about six cigarettes before his brain and body started to function again. He wondered why his conscience never traveled to conventions with him. He paid his check with the credit card he never left home without, and thought about the conscience he never left home with. Most ego trips don't care for the excess baggage of morals. Besides, he couldn't pack something he didn't have. *Everybody does it*, he said to himself as he took the receipt from the waiter. His expense reports were always well-supported by receipts, he wasn't one who would cheat the company, just one who cheated those who loved him.

Outside he paused to get his bearings, then began walking toward the beach. He saw young children playing in the sand and felt a certain nagging nostalgia that rose from the pit of his stomach whenever he came in contact with innocence. He remembered his time of youthful idealism when he was sure he could save the world; now he wasn't sure if he could save himself. He wasn't even sure he wanted to. He wasn't even sure who he was. He was just one narcissistic person among millions, and he had lost all sense of meaning deep in the darkness of his billfold and self-serving pleasure seeking.

He was a self-made man. Now, in his mind, he stood back and stared at his creation with vacant eyes, which were no longer the windows of his soul. His empty eyes gazed upon this statue he'd carved of himself. It appeared to be the shoddy work of a soul-sick sculptor, and he was aghast as the thought slowly rose to engulf him; he was the sculptor. His was modern art, having no meaning except what he chose to give it.

When he finally returned to his room to pack, he was glad the woman was gone. Soon the airplane would be taking him home where he could once again play his leading role on the hometown stage. It was too bad he couldn't pack something inside his heart because it sure was empty.

The woman shuffled into the hotel coffee shop with all the other convention cattle . . .

Par for the Course

Liar and golf are both
four letter words.

Unknown

The men standing on the first tee of the local golf course were dressed as though they had been in a head-on collision with a rainbow. Such colorful attire could get a person killed at the beer joint down the highway, but not here because this was the Country Club. They made nervous jokes, knowing soon their egos would be placed on a small wooden peg. It would be an afternoon of camaraderie, conversation, competition and a wee bit of cheating.

Some purists say you can't trust a man who hurries down the fairway alone to hunt the ball he hooked into a wooded area resembling the Amazon Forest—especially when his pockets look like a chipmunk with a mouthful of acorns. Perhaps the old shout, "I found it!" is the loudest lie in the world, with the possible exception of yelling "fore!" from the tee box to the folks on the green of the four hundred yard par four.

However, Big Earl, the club hustler, says you can't trust a man who won't cheat on the golf course. He says a man who won't cheat on the golf course will even tell your wife the exact time you left the course. Usually this is the same guy who has a telephone in his hunting cabin.

You may have seen Big Earl. He wears those shirts that have just one button—located about three inches above the belly button. He has enough chest hair to prove Darwin's theory of evolution, and wears a gold necklace large enough to double as a tire chain in the event of a sudden snow. Big Earl usually rides alone in his golf cart since he brings along two coolers of beer.

Unfortunately, this had led to him being fined by the golf committee for chemically destroying much of the foliage in the woods on the back nine. Fortunately, Big Earl wasn't one of the foursome waiting to tee off on this particularly beautiful day.

Playing in this foursome was a retired colonel, a doctor, an accountant and some guy named Vinnie, with a very crooked nose, who kept saying he could get them anything they wanted wholesale.

They spoke of graphite drivers, sore muscles, the heavyweight title fight and the great weather. Ma Bell must have loved her sons of success. In this group there were two portable phones and three beepers. Later, Big Earl would swear that one of them even had a fax machine in his golf cart. Of course nobody believed him, mainly because he said it while his face was flat on the table at the Nineteenth Hole Bar and Grill.

The colonel was the first to hit. The sun reflected off his spit-shined golf shoes as he addressed the ball. He was still so military he would complain of having a 1700 shadow when he didn't shave close enough. His drive was straight down the middle, and his proud bearing almost solicited a salute. Big Earl says the colonel is an alright guy, but doubts his habit of locating his tee shots using field glasses—especially since myopic caddies have never had a problem finding his drives.

The doctor was next to hit and he stood staring thoughtfully down the fairway. His drive was perfect. He smiled as he slowly removed the latex glove from his left hand. Big Earl says now that he has solved the tee time problem with the doctor, he loves to play golf with him. Big Earl says he simply sets his watch on PST, Physician Standard Time, which is two hours behind everyone else's time zone.

Vinnie stooped with both knees to put his tee in the ground. Usually this is an indication that it's going to be a long, long day on the golf course. Sure enough, Vinnie sliced the ball into the woods. Everyone shook their heads with that "tough luck" grimace to make him feel better. Of course, what this really means is "Why is God punishing me?" All good golfers know that "dying in vain" is when you get snake-bit while searching for someone else's ball in the woods.

The accountant was the last to hit. He teed his ball, then pulled out his yardage marker notebook as he propped his driver against his leg. Big Earl says a man who does that on a par five is probably brain dead. Anyway, the accountant adjusted his glasses, tugged up his trousers, pulled at his left sleeve, waggled his driver, then froze over the ball like a Pointer. With great precision, he hit a duck hook into the trees on the left. The golf gods smiled on him as the ball ricocheted among the trees and bounced back into the fairway about a hundred yards from the tee. He said he stayed back on his right side too long. Big Earl would have said he should have stayed back at the club house.

When the first hole was out of the way, things got better. They played 18 as though they were 18. They had a great time with a lot of camaraderie and fun. Sure there were "Mulligans" and "miraculously found" balls that were sitting up on grass pods in the woods, and maybe a few improvements of lies—both in the rough and in their stories. But so what? As Big Earl so often says, "Show me a man who is a good golfer, and I'll show you a man who takes life too seriously." Oh, by the way, Vinnie won the match. As Earl says, "Never beat a man who can get you anything wholesale."

Leaving the 18th green, the accountant moaned it was

the worst he had ever played. The colonel topped off the day with a wry smile and responded mischievously, "Oh, you've played before?"

It's a Beautiful Day in This Neighborhood

Often, when mankind cannot
change the course of events,
a kind man can.

Unknown

I hadn't watched the children's television program, Mr. Rogers, for many years. My vague memories contained images of him coming through a door on the set and putting on his sweater, taking off his street shoes and slipping into sneakers, which he neatly tied, singing, "It's a beautiful day in this neighborhood," and giving affirmations which were intended to make his small viewers feel special. There seemed to have been some teaching of elementary information, but I couldn't remember any of that.

So, in a nutshell, that's my total recall of Mr. Rogers, except I do remember being deeply impressed with his sincerity, gentleness and genuine interest in young people, which he expressed each show as he looked squarely into the camera and spoke in his quiet-mannered way. I imagine most of his young viewers thought Mr. Rogers was speaking directly to them. However, I know one *adult* viewer who knows for sure that Mr. Rogers was speaking directly to her on that turning-point-afternoon in her life. Her name is Katherine. She told me her story several years ago. It's the kind of story that I'll never forget—it's too unique and poignant for forgetting to take place.

On her turning-point-day, Katherine was sitting cross-legged on the floor right in front of her television. Her two young boys would usually be flanking her as Mr. Rogers came on, but this afternoon they were at her mother's house.

So Katherine was alone as she turned the set on with a feeble push of her finger. Although she had recently turned 30, her long hair tied in a ponytail made her look like the proverbial girl next door. She had made special arrangements to insure her boys wouldn't be with her. She wanted to spare them the impending terror borne from the shame that had been living next door to her soul, crowding out any semblance of self-love. Katherine wanted nothing in life but out.

For weeks, her once sky-bright blue eyes had been full of dark clouds and drizzling rain. Katherine's smile, which was usually as broad as the Mississippi, had dried up until not even a faint trickle seeped across her lips. Depression and drugs had stolen her soul's energy and emotion until, finally, too tired to wander aimlessly from room to room, she had eased herself down to the floor in front of the television. This afternoon she was holding a loaded gun instead of her two children.

Who knows how these tragic moments come about? For Katherine, this behavior made perfect sense. She had lost her job as a nurse because she had become addicted to narcotics. The narcotics crept into her life following a back injury she had suffered at the doctor's office where she worked. She had been caught forging the doctor's name on narcotics prescriptions, and he had fired her instead of prosecuting.

Katherine felt so much shame, so much guilt, so much fear, and her sadness filled the entire den where she now sat. Like most desperate people, she had had those fraternal twin thoughts of suicide and salvation all morning, and this afternoon suicide had become the favored child.

Yesterday she was raising children, now she was raising the gun to her head, her finger on the trigger. Through tears she saw the painfully gentle face of Mr. Rogers as his so-kind voice spoke directly to her. "You're a good person. Everybody is special, and I like you just the way you are," Mr. Rogers said, as his finger pointed toward Katherine. There was no doubt in her mind. Katherine knew for certain he was speaking to her. Mr. Rogers was an old special friend. His sincere message was that no matter what was happening, she was special and that he liked her just the way she was.

The suicidal spell was broken, but Katherine no longer was. She began regaining a grip on herself while releasing the grip on the trigger. Her shaking hand placed the gun on top of the television as Mr. Rogers' face smiled back at her and sang, ". . . I'll be back when the day is new, we'll have lots of things to do, you'll have things you'll want to talk about, I will too." Oh, yes, indeed he would see her tomorrow.

Strange how God works. That was the turning-point afternoon when Katherine surrendered her self-hate and self-destruction to Mr. Rogers.

God bless you and thank you Mr. Rogers. Thought you'd like to know just how special you are, and how truly special my favorite friend Katherine has become. Because of you, it really is a beautiful day in this neighborhood.

Not All Children Are Afraid of Thunder

Faith is to believe what
you do not yet see; the reward
for this faith is to see
what you believe.

Saint Augustine

Nine-year-old Davy rolled his wheelchair up to the screened door of the weathered trailer, which sat perched on a hill about 50 feet from the two lane country road below. He looked. The road was empty. Two red balloons tied to the mailbox were motionless in the still Mississippi August morning.

All morning, his arms made stronger with anticipation, Davy had pushed himself back and forth between the screened door and the Saturday morning cartoons on the old black and white television. Soon they would be coming. That's what his daddy had said, but Davy knew his father often had a big voice that was small on truth. Still, Davy wanted to believe. One thing was certain, Davy was a true believer if ever there was one.

"Are you sure they knew this was the day they were supposed to come, Daddy?" Davy asked.

"I told you, boy, they'll be here," his father answered as he sat up on the sofa, stretched, and finished off his third beer of the morning.

"Get me another beer, boy," his father said, as he rubbed his unshaven face.

"Yes sir," Davy replied, rolling his chair across the cracked linoleum floor into the kitchen.

"Mom, Dad wants another beer," Davy said as the TV blared away. Davy's mom frowned, then opened the refrigerator and handed him a cold can, which he pressed against his face.

"It sure is going to be a hot one today," she said with the special smile she always gave to him. She, like the trailer, looked worn and weathered, but somehow she too managed to keep on standing up. She wasn't a quitter. If she had been, she would have left years ago, but she knew without her Davy wouldn't have much of a chance.

"They are coming, aren't they, Mom?" Davy asked, seeking reassurance from the one person he knew would be honest with him.

"I don't know for sure, honey," she said wiping the grease from the rusty stove top, "We'll just have to wait and see."

There were some things that Davy's mom did know for sure. Davy had muscular dystrophy and a recent diagnosis of leukemia. She had borrowed money from her brother so she could send Davy to the summer camp for handicapped children. That was the one thing Davy had talked all summer about wanting to do. She didn't know if Davy would even be around next summer, so she borrowed the money which she sent directly to the camp to make sure Davy's father would have no chance of squandering it.

"You know what, Mom? I think I love Harley motorcycles more than anything in the world." His eyes shone behind his words.

"I know you do, sweetheart," she said, as she straightened the red Harley bandana on his forehead and tugged down on his little denim jacket.

Davy's mom had prayed they would come. A month ago, her husband had printed the message on a plain sheet of paper and taken it to the local Harley shop. It read: *Davy's Ride For Life. Nine year old boy with Muskuler Distrofree and Loukemia going to camp. Desirs Harly s-cort to camp. Come at 8:00 A.M., August 17th. P.S. wants to ride to camp in semi-tralor two if possible.* The rural address was printed at the bottom.

"You better get that beer to your daddy," she whispered, and as Davy wheeled back into the tiny living room she was thankful she had remembered to gas up their old truck just in case nobody showed up. It was over a hundred miles from their trailer to the camp for special children.

Davy rolled to a stop at the end of the sofa, handed his daddy the beer can, then asked, "Are you sure they'll be here, Daddy? It's after 8:00 and you said they'd be here at 8:00. Mamma said I had to be at camp by 11:00 to sign in."

"Listen, boy," his daddy said in his loud voice, "I told you this was the day your wheelchair would be your throne and you would be the king of the day. Now you go back to that door and keep looking." His daddy's drooping eyes returned to the TV. Davy knew the conversation was over.

Davy pushed his wheelchair back over to the screen door. His arms didn't feel as strong as earlier. He sure wanted to be king for the day. Oh, my, how he loved Harleys and big trucks. Right now he wanted to believe he was more than a nine-year-old muscular dystrophy child confined to a wheelchair, so he kept the faith and his morning vigilance at the screen door.

Davy looked down from the door, but still the road was empty. The hot August sun had baked off the dew, and the searing heat had already begun making road mirages shimmer in the distance. Still, he kept the faith.

Davy's mom hurried from the kitchen. Abruptly, she reached the TV and shut it off. "Listen!" she said with wide eyes, "Do ya'll hear that thunder?"

"What are you yelling about, woman?" Davy's dad demanded gruffly, "It's hot as hell. That's just heat thunder, woman. Turn the TV back on."

Suddenly, Davy screamed as loud as he could, "Pick me up, Daddy, pick me up!"

"Hell, boy, you ain't scared of a little thunder are you?" he asked.

"Pick me up, Daddy. Please carry me outside," he pleaded.

Davy's mom didn't wait for her husband to respond. She rushed past him to the wheelchair, hoisted Davy into her arms, shoved the screen door open and carried him out onto the small concrete slab at the top of the steps.

Davy's father was wrong about the thunder. Another thing he didn't know was that his handwritten message had set into motion fate and forces far from the run-down trailer. The local Harley dealer had typed the handwritten message and sent it to every dealer in Florida, Alabama, Mississippi, Louisiana and Texas. The dealer had been specific: Travel Interstate 10. Harleys will join up at every rest stop along the way. Groups coming from the east and west will meet at 7:30 A.M. at Mississippi Highway 47 exit headed north.

Oh, Davy's mom had heard right. It was thunder for sure, but it was a unique rolling thunder. That special one-of-a-kind sound that only comes when large numbers of Harleys are traveling together. The wait was over. They were coming.

The first thing Davy saw coming over the crest of the hill on the shimmering road was the biggest, most beautiful gleaming tractor trailer in the whole world. It was no mirage, it was his miracle. Once the huge rig cleared the crest, Davy started laughing and crying at the same time. He could not believe what he saw. Neither could his mom or even his daddy.

Stretched out behind the big rig as far as his eyes could see were over 700 Harley Davidson motorcycles. They had come to escort the tractor trailer in which Davy would be riding to the special summer camp.

It was as though Davy was going to Heaven and the Harleys were angels sent to carry him home. It was the most magnificent sight and sound he had ever experienced. God surely works in mysterious ways.

In February of the following year, Davy died. Surely God sent as many real angels to escort Davy to Heaven.

Doubting Thomas

Faith is the substance of
things hoped for, the evidence
of things not seen.

Hebrews 11:1

It was Christmas Eve. Edward Thomas pulled out of the truck stop. He was heading home. His stomach and his Mercedes were both full. He had a trunk-load of presents. Home was five hours away. He headed toward the on ramp of the interstate. Life was good.

As he drove down the ramp leading back onto the interstate, he noticed a man leaning against the guard rail on the shoulder of the road. The man's posture reminded Thomas of a question mark: His skinny body arched forward with his head looking down at the ground. It was almost dark and the temperature was dropping. He turned on the heater.

He adjusted his rear view mirror as he drove past the man. His eyes caught a glimpse of the thin old figure just as it crumpled face down onto the pavement. Thomas hesitated a moment as if his foot couldn't decide between the gas or the brake pedal. The gas belonged to the hurrying Santa, while the brake beckoned the reluctant Samaritan to stop. Right before entering the interstate his foot found the brake. Reluctantly, he backed up the shoulder of the ramp.

He got out of his car and cautiously approached the old man who was not moving. Ten feet away from him Thomas stopped and yelled, "Are you all right?"

No answer came from the fallen body. He moved closer, thinking the man was probably just a drunk who had passed out. He knelt down beside the lifeless figure and shook him. Still, there was no response. Thomas smelled no alcohol when he rolled the thin man over onto his back. The old man weakly opened his eyes and looked up at him.

"What's wrong with you?" Thomas asked, in a too-loud voice as two cars sped past them down the ramp. Thomas wanted nothing more than to have another car stop and relieve him of the unwanted responsibility of helping this dried out prune of a man lying on the pavement. No cars stopped.

The old man whispered through his whiskers, "Thank you for stopping. I'm just tired and hungry. Guess I must have passed out. I think I'll be okay if you just help me to my feet."

Thomas pulled him to his feet as though he were weightless. He went through the motions of dusting dirt and gravel off the old man's worn top coat.

"Are you going to be okay?" Thomas asked, knowing the old man would say "Yes," even though the reality was "No." He hated himself for being as cold as the weather, but he had done enough to soothe his conscience and was ready to go.

The gray bearded wisp of a man didn't respond to that question. Instead, he leveled his eyes at Edward Thomas and asked, "What time is it?" It was a question that was asked with urgency.

Thomas immediately pushed the light button on his Rolex watch. "It's six o'clock," Thomas replied, but the pride in his expensive possession was strangely absent.

"Then we must hurry," the grizzled man said as he grabbed Thomas's arm with one frail hand as the other pointed toward the night sky. "We have to follow that bright star over there. That's the star sent to guide us to the child of God."

Thomas was startled. *My God!* he thought, *This old man is crazy*. He quickly pulled his arm away from the gaunt man's weak grasp.

"Don't be afraid," the old man said quickly, "Surely you are one of the wise men sent to follow the star. I knew you would come. Surely you are a wise man, for you value people more than possessions. Why else would you be here?"

Thomas suddenly felt ashamed. It was almost a forgotten feeling for him. Apologetically he said, "I'm sorry, I really must go."

The question mark of an old man now stood erect like an exclamation mark as he exclaimed, "Edward, we must hurry! The star is near. Forget your trunk load of presents and your fancy watch, but don't forget you are one of the chosen wise men."

The cold night air rushed into Thomas's open mouth. He stood stunned. "How did you . . ." The question was drowned out in the roar of a huge tractor trailer barreling down the ramp.

The smiling old man didn't wait for him to repeat it. "Are you coming, Edward?" he asked as he began walking toward the car.

"Uh, uh, yes," Edward answered, then hurried after him.

After they had traveled several miles on the interstate, Edward turned toward the old man and asked, "Can I get you some food?"

"There's no time," came the old man's reply as he continued to look out the window. "Look! There's the star! Turn off at the next exit. We're almost there!"

As they were coming up the off ramp, Edward saw the bright star too. They went down a paved country road and took a left on a dirt road until finally the dusty Mercedes came to a stop in front of a shack directly beneath the bright star. "This is it!" cried the old man, "Hurry! Let's go see the Child of God!" he yelled as he opened the car door.

At first Edward was hesitant, then he found himself caught up in the old man's excitement, and he rushed after him. The cry of a baby pierced the silence of the night.

The occupants of the shack seemed to know the old man, and once inside the shack the two men found a beautiful baby lying in the arms of a very innocent but poor-looking young woman.

Edward shyly stood in the doorway as the old man rushed to the bedside and knelt. Then he pulled something from his pocket and placed it in the hand of the mother. The old man looked back over at Edward and smiled. Edward suddenly remembered the presents in the car and went outside. He returned in a moment with a beautiful stuffed toy for the baby boy. Edward felt an eerie chill run through him as he knelt down beside the bed and placed the toy in the hand of the mother. Without a word the old man rose to his feet and motioned for Edward to follow him. It was time to leave.

Once outside and in the car, Edward slowly came to his senses. They drove down the dirt road back toward the paved road.

"Where do you want me to drop you off?" Edward Thomas asked.

"At the paved road," came the old man's gentle reply.

"How did you know . . ." Edward started to ask but was interrupted by the old man.

"Well, I know you wonder, don't you Edward, how I knew those things about you? Well, I saw your personalized license tag and a slip of wrapping paper stuck in the bottom of your trunk lid. And, believe it or not, I have seen a Rolex watch before. So really it was nothing but simple deduction."

"But who are you?" Edward asked.

"Me? I'm just an old country doctor who lives in this

county. You see, I'm too old to drive any more and I had to deliver some medicine to that new mother back there. I came down the highway because I figured someone kind like you would give me a ride if I stood on the edge of the road long enough."

"But you tricked me!" Edward burst out. "You lied. You said you were a wise man who was going to follow the bright star to find the Child of God."

The old man laughed a lovely laugh. "Edward, don't you get it? We are wise men because we know there are billions of stars; therefore, each person must be born beneath one. But above all," the old doctor said smiling, "we both know that everyone is a child of God. Isn't that great?"

Edward nodded his head "yes" toward the old doctor whose eyes now twinkled even brighter than the stars. "I think I see what you mean," Edward said as the car came to a stop at the pavement. "Merry Christmas, Doc," Edward said as the old man opened the door.

"It always is when you are a wise man, Edward Thomas," the old man said.

"How did you know my last . . ." The door closed and the old man vanished into the field across the paved road.

Edward Thomas drove home singing Christmas carols without a doubt.

A Song for
Unsung Heroes

Many prisoners of war are
never captured.

Unknown

Byron was a high school friend. He was different from us, but we liked him anyway. Byron was already marching to the beat of a distant drummer, while we sat absent-mindedly thumping our pencils on initial-scarred desks.

Byron made straight As in tough courses, not foot stools in woodworking; played the piano, not hooky; ran for school president, not touchdowns; read poetry instead of pornography; oil painted in place of changing oil; shot photographs of birds instead of shooting them; quoted lines from Shakespeare, not lewd limericks; drank in knowledge, not beer; knew more about church than "churchkeys;" wrote on Wordsworth, not bathroom walls; and smiled his sweet smile whenever we called him a "momma's boy."

Byron was always growing in culture, while the only culture we had growing was beneath our uncut fingernails. In retrospect it's easy to see he was already brilliant, while we were still quite barbaric. He was a gentle boy who grew into a gentle man. In fact, an officer and a gentleman.

Byron was a scholar who received a full scholarship to Harvard. We dumb "jocks" thought perhaps the Ivy League had something to do with baseball. Our ignorance couldn't save us as graduation hurled us from the halcyon halls of high school to the alarm of life's fire drill. It was a time when Thomas Wolfe's statement, "You can't go home again," was merely an obscure quotation on an English test.

187

Years and friendships drifted away. Trying to get in touch with ourselves, we lost touch with each other; we migrated like birds seeking the sunny promised land.

Mr. Anthony, who owned the neighborhood grocery store, remained the common point, the liaison, of our various lives. He had watched us grow up. He asked about our identities, not our identification as they do nowadays. His concern for people ran deeper than their pocketbooks, and he was a ready resource to fill you in on "whatever became of so and so." Any trips back to the old neighborhood usually included a stop at Mr. Anthony's store for the current update.

Surprisingly, Mr. Anthony recognized me even after several years absence. He still had that knack of "fishing" around with questions until he yanked your good qualities up from the muddy pools of yourself, and then made you feel like they should be mounted on a trophy wall. When he finished finding out how I was doing, he asked me if I had heard about poor Byron. When I heard the word "poor," I knew bad news would follow. It did.

Mr. Anthony said Byron had become an officer in the Army and had been sent to Vietnam, where he had fought bravely until he was wounded by enemy rifle fire. Mr. Anthony had spoken with Byron's mother several times, and she'd told him about the medals and commendations that Byron had received. She said Byron didn't leave the house very often, and she'd appreciate it if Mr. Anthony would tell some of Byron's old high school friends to come by and see him if any of us ever came by the store. Mr. Anthony urged me to go see him. I promised I would.

The houses on Division Avenue looked smaller than I remembered as I drove toward Byron's house. This was a reluctant reunion pursued more out of respect than friendship. Nine years had passed and a strange awkwardness engulfed me. Memory lane had become overgrown and tangled with the brambles of time and separation until it resembled the old trails on Red Mountain, which were now obliterated by kudzu. I arrived at Byron's.

Byron's mother was as gracious as ever and led me back to the dimly lit den where Byron sat with the blinds closed. Then she politely busied herself so we could be alone.

Byron was a straw man stranger sitting in the shadows. The substance he once had was absent; he had become a "hollow" man with empty eyes.

He said he had no permanent injuries from the war. With slurred words, he spoke of the oddity of fighting for foreign independence, while he himself had become dependent on narcotics until he was now foreign to himself.

Byron was a heroin addict; a hero slowly dying from shooting his dead father's inheritance through the veins in his body. He nodded off and I said my good-byes to his mom.

The front door closed behind me. I knew the truth. Byron was never captured, yet he was a prisoner of war just the same. In a supreme paradox, Byron died from his heroin dependency by overdosing on July 4th, 1970.

There are many heroes to be honored with Independence Day fireworks and parades. Yet, in my mind, there are untold numbers of heroes who quietly line the streets. They are those recovering addicts and alcoholics who have fought bravely for independence from drug dependency. They understand that the most dangerous battlefield is in our minds, and winning the war that rages inside of us is a heroic achievement.

Addiction demeans our lives. Life has to be more than pacing back and forth, waiting for death to enter the door.

To those recovering people—whether the addiction was food, alcohol, drugs, cigarettes, gambling or whatever—Happy Independence Day to you.

Starving Souls

The hunger of the stomach
is mild when compared to the
gnawing hunger of
the heart.

Unknown

T he line formed early outside the Downtown Mission. It was Thanksgiving Day and the cold northeastern wind brought quick shivers and the loitering smells of food being cooked in the old brick building. Hungry homeless humans stretched around the block. Dressed in shabby, ill-fitting clothes, they shifted from one foot to the other trying to stay warm.

From the window on the seventh floor of the office building across the street, the long line resembled a gigantic molting snake trying to shake loose from its shedding skin. The man standing at the window stared down at the surrealistic human serpent. He gazed on with much the same kind of detachment that one has when flying over an area where great destruction has occurred. The devastation is real but the distance makes it almost impossible to fully understand what the scene means in terms of human tragedy. So it was with the man in the window.

He saw the people below but he didn't feel anything. They didn't seem real. They weren't people down on their luck; they were more like raisins, no longer plump and full, but shriveled and dried up. "Can't make a grape out of a raisin," he thought to himself as his hands felt the coldness of the window. The thought seemed to satisfy his conscience which was just about the only satisfaction he had felt recently.

November had brought a strange numbness which he couldn't understand or shake. It had blunted his senses, while taking the zest and meaning from his life. He felt

so isolated that for a moment he almost envied the close-
ness of the people in the line who were waiting to be fed.
As he watched them, he kept switching his weight from
one foot to the other, but was totally unaware of his imi-
tative gesture.

Below, an old man and his dog stood together in line.
The dog's coat was as tattered and mangy-looking as his
master's. The dog leaned against the old man's leg. They
provided warmth and support for each other. Even their
scraggly bodies bonded them together in appearance.
They were quite a pair, but at least they were a pair.

"Won't be long now, Harry," the old man said to the
dog. "Just like last year," he almost whispered, as the dog
looked up at him. "A turkey drumstick, mashed potatoes,
dressing, cranberry sauce and a roll big as my fist." The
old man doubled his scrawny hand into a fist then
shoved it deep down into his pocket. Harry let out a
knowing whine that said even dogs know the universal
language of hunger.

"You know what, Harry?" The old man asked and then
waited as though Harry might possibly answer. "When
we get that plate of food we're not even going to take it
back to the house," he said, referring to their cardboard
box nestled beneath the railroad trestle where they slept.
"I'm going to take that foil off that food and we'll eat it
right here on the street. Just you and me." Harry barked
as he heard the excitement in his master's voice.

The line moved forward as the Mission began handing
out the Thanksgiving dinners, which were served on
paper plates and wrapped in aluminum foil.

"Hey, Harry," the old man sputtered, "I almost forgot to
tell you. Somebody told me they heard Mr. Paul Harvey,
that news guy, say that 50 percent of the people in this
country are only two paychecks away from being

homeless. Can you believe it, Harry?" Harry cocked his head to one side as the old man continued. "A lot of people got no money cushion at all. Any folks losing their jobs these days are in big trouble. Ain't that something, Harry?" he questioned again as the line lurched forward once more.

The seventh floor window slid open. The man standing there didn't feel the cold air rushing in; in fact, he didn't feel anything. He placed one leg up on the window sill and the wind whipped his pants leg. His body leaned precariously out the window.

The plate of food warmed the old man's hands as he and Harry scurried over to the curb. The old man balanced the food in both hands as he plopped down on the curb. "I told you Harry! Didn't I tell you Harry? We're going to have Thanksgiving right here." Harry sat down beside his master with more obedience than can be formally taught as the old man picked up the drumstick. The dog's eyes were as watery from the cold wind as his master's. The old man, not aware of his own eyes, hesitated as he looked at Harry. It was as though he were seeing him for the first time. "Don't cry Harry! Here, you can have this drumstick," he said as he wiped Harry's eyes with his dirty handkerchief then began to break the meat away from the bone and feed Harry, who gently nuzzled the food from his hand.

"You stupid old fool!" screamed the man from the open window on the seventh floor. "Why are you feeding that dumb dog, you fool?" he bellowed down as he leaned dangerously further out of the window with hands cupped like a megaphone around his mouth.

The old man stood up, cupped his own hands around his mouth, and let out a scream that came somewhere from deep inside his twisted soul. "Because he's starving!"

The words rose like frightened birds and soared up to the man on the seventh floor. Refusing to die they echoed down the concrete corridor formed by the tall office buildings. "He's starving . . . starving . . . starving!"

Falling down from the seventh floor came words too bitter and heavy for the man in the window to hold. "Who's going to feed you, you old fool? Who needs you anyway?"

The old man softly shrugged his shoulders and pointed toward Harry. Then he lifted his right arm straight up over his head until his finger pointed toward the heavens, then he slowly lowered it until it was directed toward the man now squatting in the window. The man sat frozen on the sill as the old man's hand turned over until it was open and beckoning.

The pleading hand was louder than words. The well-dressed man in the window was wealthy. He would never be one of Paul Harvey's statistics. He was rich, but alone. He was used to engraved RSVPs. But never in his life had he received such a sincere invitation.

The man's face looked as if he had just awakened from some awful nightmare. Cautiously, he now eased himself back into his office. He leaned his head back outside and said, "I'm coming down."

He closed the window and went down to the street in a much different way than he had originally planned. Some hungers are stronger than the hunger for food. This man's hunger would soon be fed by a homeless old man and his dog.

As the changed man came toward them, the old man looked up at the building, then back down at his dog as he whispered, "See, Harry, the seventh floor ain't too high for angels to fly."

About the Author

John M. Eades, Ph.D., resides in Mobile, Alabama, but he is a native of Birmingham. He received his Ph.D. in counseling from the University of Alabama in 1980.

Dr. Eades has done post-graduate work at the University of Georgia, Harvard University and the Johnson Institute, all in the field of addiction.

Dr. Eades is presently the Director of Chemical Dependency Services for the Singing River Hospital System in Pascagoula, Mississippi. He is a 20-year veteran in the field of addictive disease counseling and has served as chemical dependency director for several major hospitals. He has also been involved in private practice as a therapist treating a wide range of psychological, emotional and behavioral problems.

Dr. Eades' experience with addicts and his understanding of human behavior has led him to write articles for hospital newsletters as well as for *The Mississippi Press* in Pascagoula. He is an accomplished public speaker and has addressed numerous conventions and professional organizations as he strives to bring inspiration and humor to the many topics he covers in his presentations.

Dr. Eades has been married for 32 years and is the father of two grown daughters.

Your feedback and reaction to this book would be appreciated. Please send your comments to:

John M. Eades
3151 Ward Road
Mobile, AL 36605
(334) 476-8389

Lectures, Addiction Seminars, Speaking Engagements

John M. Eades, Ph.D., would be pleased to come share his knowledge about addictions, especially gambling addiction.

Inspirational, motivational and humorous presentations are available. Please contact him at the above address.